GCSE English

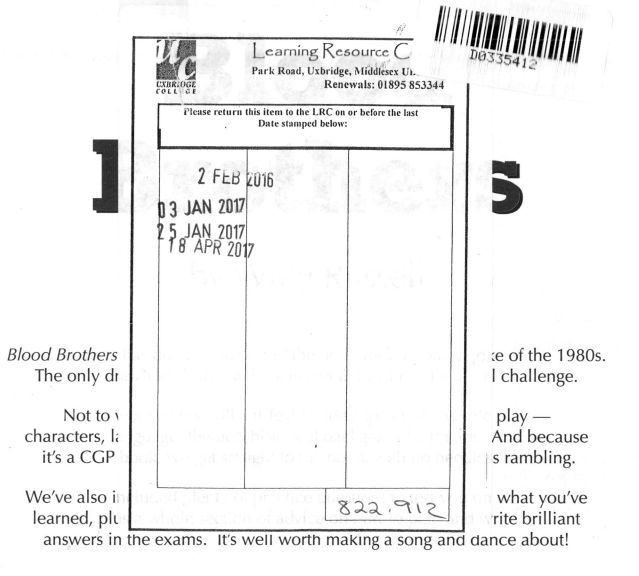
Blood Brothers _____ ce of the 1980s.
The only d_____ l challenge.

Not to _____ play —
characters, l_____ And because
it's a CGP _____ s rambling.

We've also i_____ what you've
learned, plu_____ write brilliant
answers in the exams. It's well worth making a song and dance about!

The Text Guide

CONTENTS

CONTENTS

The Characters in 'Blood Brothers'
'Blood Brothers' Cartoon

Published by CGP

Editors:
Emma Bonney
Claire Boulter
Ben Ffrancon Davies

Contributor:
Jane Harrison

With thanks to Matt Topping and Nicola Woodfin for the proofreading.
With thanks to Jan Greenway for the copyright research.

Acknowledgements:
With thanks to Mary Evans Picture Library for permission to use the images on pages 1, 2 & 7

With thanks to Rex Features for permission to use the images on pages 1, 3, 20, 21, 28, 29, 30, 35, 40, 47 & 48

With thanks to Photostage.co.uk for permission to use the images on the cover and on pages 3, 4, 5, 10, 11, 12, 15, 16, 22, 24, 26, 27, 34, 36, 37, 39, 41, 45 & 50

With thanks to Lisa Bowerman Photography for permission to use the images on pages 3, 5, 13, 14, 17, 23, 25, 38, 44, 46 & 49

With thanks to Alamy for permission to use the images on pages 6 & 8

Every effort has been made to locate copyright holders and obtain permission to reproduce sources.
For those sources where it has been difficult to trace the copyright holder of the work, we would be grateful
for information. If any copyright holder would like us to make an amendment to the acknowledgements,
please notify us and we will gladly update the book at the next reprint. Thank you.

ISBN: 978 1 78294 311 2
Printed by Elanders Ltd, Newcastle upon Tyne.
Clipart from Corel®

Based on the classic CGP style created by Richard Parsons.

Introduction to 'Blood Brothers' and Willy Russell

'Blood Brothers' is about social class and identity

- *Blood Brothers* is a play about <u>twin brothers</u>, one of whom (Edward) is <u>secretly given away</u> at birth.

- Edward is raised in a <u>middle-class</u> family, whilst his twin (Mickey) is raised by their <u>working-class</u> mother.

- Willy Russell uses Mickey and Edward to explore ideas about how <u>social class</u> affects people's lives.

The play reflects the society of the time

1) The play was written in the <u>early 1980s</u>, but it's set sometime between the <u>1960s</u> and <u>1980s</u>.

2) There was a strong <u>class divide</u> in Britain at this time. The middle classes had more opportunities than the working classes. This was reflected in things like education, job prospects and wealth.

3) The characters in the play are <u>fictional</u>, but they are used to comment on this <u>class divide</u>.

© Mary Evans Picture Library/Shirley Baker

Willy Russell writes about class divides

- Russell was born into a <u>working-class</u> family. His father had various jobs, including mining and factory work. His mother worked as a nurse and later in a warehouse.

- He grew up near <u>Liverpool</u>, where many of his plays are set.

- His plays focus on the problems faced by <u>working-class</u> people. He writes a lot about <u>social divides</u> and how someone's <u>class</u> can affect who they are.

1947	Born in Whiston, near <u>Liverpool</u>.
1963	Left school aged <u>15</u> to work as a hairdresser.
1967	Returned to full-time education and trained as a <u>teacher</u>.
1971	Wrote his <u>first play</u>, 'Keep Your Eyes Down' while still a teacher.
1981	Wrote '<u>Blood Brothers</u>' as a <u>play</u>. He adapted it into a <u>musical</u> the following year.
1984	Nominated for an <u>Academy Award</u> for the screenplay for 'Educating Rita'.
1988	Revival of 'Blood Brothers' opened in the <u>West End</u>.
2012	'Blood Brothers' closed after a <u>24-year</u> run, making it the third longest-running musical ever performed in the West End.

© Maggie Hardie/REX

Background Information

'Blood Brothers' is set in Liverpool and Skelmersdale

Act One takes place in Liverpool and Act Two takes place in Skelmersdale
— a town to the <u>northeast</u> of the city. Here are the <u>key locations</u> in the play:

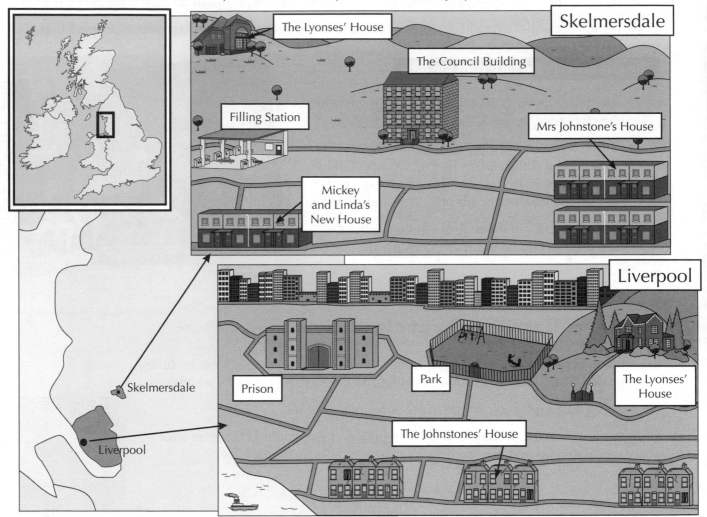

Both locations are home to middle-class and working-class people

- Liverpool and Skelmersdale both have <u>working-class</u> and <u>middle-class</u> areas.

- In <u>Liverpool</u>, there was a lot of <u>poor quality</u> housing for the working classes, often close to the docks or factories where they worked. The middle classes lived in more <u>affluent</u> parts of the city, with plenty of green space.

- <u>Skelmersdale</u> was a <u>New Town</u> (see p.8). Many working-class Liverpool residents were <u>rehoused</u> there in the 1960s. There were already people living in Skelmersdale, including <u>middle-class</u> families.

Introduction

Who's Who in 'Blood Brothers'

Mrs Johnstone...

...is Mickey, Edward and Sammy's mother. She gives Edward up so he'll have a better life.

Mrs Lyons...

...is a middle-class woman who longs for a child. She manipulates Mrs Johnstone into giving Edward to her.

Mickey Johnstone...

...is the twin Mrs Johnstone keeps. He's a friendly child but ends up unemployed and in trouble with the law.

Edward Lyons...

...is the twin Mrs Lyons takes. He's well-educated and grows up to be a successful local councillor.

Linda...

...is Mickey and Edward's friend. Both boys fall in love with her, and she marries Mickey.

Sammy Johnstone...

...is Mickey's older brother. He's always in trouble as a child and ends up as a criminal.

Mr Lyons...

...is a wealthy businessman who spends more time at work than with his family. He makes Mickey redundant.

The Narrator...

...helps to tell the story. He also plays several minor characters throughout the play.

Chorus Members...

...sing parts of the story and play some minor characters, such as the 'Dole-ites'.

Introduction

'Blood Brothers' — Plot Summary

© Donald Cooper/ Photostage.co.uk

'Blood Brothers'... what happens when?

Here's a little recap of the <u>main events</u> of 'Blood Brothers'. It's a good idea to learn <u>what happens when</u>, so that in the exam you can show the examiner you know exactly what you're talking about.

Act One — The twins are born and separated

* The Narrator introduces the twins and gives an <u>overview</u> of the story. We see a <u>preview</u> of the play's final moments — Mickey and Edward <u>both die</u>.

* Mrs Johnstone sings about how her husband left her with <u>seven children</u> and she <u>can't afford</u> to feed them.

© Donald Cooper/Photostage.co.uk

* Mrs Johnstone goes to clean at Mrs Lyons' house. Mrs Lyons reveals that she and her husband <u>can't have children</u>.

* Mrs Johnstone finds out she is <u>pregnant</u> with twins. Mrs Lyons <u>persuades</u> her to give her one of the babies.

* The babies are born. Debt collectors <u>repossess</u> Mrs Johnstone's belongings. Mrs Lyons <u>takes</u> one of the babies.

* Mrs Lyons <u>fires</u> Mrs Johnstone, and tells her that both boys will <u>die</u> if they ever find out they are twins.

Act One — The boys meet, aged seven, and are separated again

* Mickey and Edward <u>meet</u> near Mickey's house. They <u>bond immediately</u>.

* Mrs Johnstone is <u>horrified</u> when she realises who Mickey's new friend is. She tells Edward to <u>leave</u> and not to come back.

* Mickey goes to see Edward but Mrs Lyons sends him away. Edward is <u>angry</u> and uses <u>swear words</u> he learnt from Mickey. Mrs Lyons <u>hits</u> him.

* Edward <u>sneaks out</u> to play with Mickey and Linda.

* Mrs Lyons tells her husband that they need to <u>move away</u>, but he's <u>unconvinced</u>. Soon afterwards, a policeman catches Edward, Mickey and Linda <u>misbehaving</u>, which persuades Mr Lyons to move his family.

* Edward goes to Mrs Johnstone's house <u>upset</u> about moving. She gives him a <u>locket</u> with a picture of her and Mickey in it.

* The Johnstones find out that they're being moved to <u>Skelmersdale</u>.

© Donald Cooper/Photostage.co.uk

Introduction

Act Two — The boys meet again as teenagers

- The Johnstones are <u>happier</u> in Skelmersdale.

- Edward is <u>suspended</u> from his boarding school. Mickey and Linda are <u>suspended</u> from their comprehensive school.

- Back home, Mickey and Edward meet and <u>recognise</u> each other. They <u>renew</u> their friendship.

- Mrs Lyons sees the boys together. She tries to <u>bribe</u> Mrs Johnstone to <u>move away</u>. When she refuses, Mrs Lyons tries to <u>attack</u> her with a knife.

- Mickey, Edward and Linda meet up and the play moves through scenes in which they age from 14 to 18.

- Edward reveals his <u>love</u> for Linda, but then <u>encourages Mickey</u> to ask her out. Edward <u>leaves</u> for university.

- Mickey and Linda get married because Linda is <u>pregnant</u>. Mickey loses his job and has to go on the <u>dole</u>.

- Edward comes home from university. Mickey <u>resents</u> him and they <u>fall out</u>.

- Edward asks Linda to <u>marry</u> him. Linda <u>admits</u> she has feelings for him, but tells him she's married to Mickey.

- Sammy <u>persuades</u> Mickey to act as lookout for a robbery, but it goes <u>wrong</u> and Sammy <u>shoots</u> the petrol station attendant. Mickey's sentenced to <u>seven years</u> in prison. He becomes <u>depressed</u> and is put on <u>pills</u>.

Act Two — The boys are now adults

- Mickey is released <u>early</u> but he is still depressed. Linda begs him to <u>stop</u> taking the pills.

- Linda gets them a <u>new house</u> and a <u>job</u> for Mickey. Mickey knows that Edward, who is now a <u>local councillor</u>, is responsible for both.

- Linda and Edward <u>kiss</u>. Meanwhile, Mickey <u>stops</u> taking his pills.

- <u>Mrs Lyons</u> shows Mickey that Edward and Linda are <u>together</u>.

- Mickey takes Sammy's gun and goes to <u>confront</u> Edward at the Town Hall.

- Mrs Johnstone tells the boys they are <u>brothers</u>. Mickey loses control and accidentally <u>shoots</u> <u>Edward</u>. The police <u>shoot Mickey</u> in response.

One thing's for sure — it ends with a bang...

So *Blood Brothers* is the story of separated twin boys brought up in different social classes. Make sure you know the plot really well before you go on to Section One — read this summary again or take a look at the cartoon at the back of the book.

Introduction

Section One — Background and Context

Britain in the Late Twentieth Century

It's a good idea to know a bit about what was happening in Britain at the time when *Blood Brothers* is set. The events of the play are shaped by the important issues of the time, such as <u>social class</u> and <u>industrial unrest</u>.

The play is set some time between the 1960s and 1980s

1) There are references throughout the play which suggest that the action is happening some time during the <u>1960s</u> and <u>1970s</u>. For example, Mr Lyons refers to the "shrinking pound" and the rising "price of oil" — real issues which affected people in the late 1960s and early 1970s.

2) Russell was also influenced by what was happening in the <u>early 1980s</u>, when he was <u>writing</u> *Blood Brothers*. Issues such as rising unemployment and recession (see p.7) are reflected in the play.

The 1960s saw the emergence of 'youth culture'

1) 'Teenagers' became a properly <u>recognised</u> age group in the 1960s. For the first time, it was widely accepted that young people had their own <u>culture</u> and ways of behaving, which made them different from both children and adults.

2) The term '<u>youth culture</u>' referred to the <u>behaviour</u> and <u>interests</u> of teenagers, including fashion, music and hobbies. Youth culture was associated with <u>freedom</u> and <u>potential</u>.

3) Bands like <u>The Beatles</u> (who came from Liverpool) had huge teenage fan bases, and their music represented feelings of being <u>young</u> and <u>carefree</u>.

4) Young people also became an <u>important force</u> in protest movements against things like nuclear weapons. They believed in their <u>power</u> to shape the future, and started to break away from their parents' views.

> **Theme — Childhood and Growing Up**
>
> Mickey, Edward and Linda's <u>teenage years</u> are presented in a very <u>positive light</u> in the play. A quick sequence of scenes show them going out together to places like the beach and the rifle range. The Narrator emphasises how <u>carefree</u> they are at this time.

> Young people often <u>imitated</u> characters from films and television. In the play, the children pretend to be cowboys, Indians and gangsters.

5) The rise of <u>mass advertising</u> and <u>colour television</u> meant that even children were <u>exposed</u> to things like films, television programmes and celebrities in a way they hadn't been before.

Family structure was still very traditional

1) The late twentieth century is often seen as a time of <u>great social change</u>.

2) There were some big developments in <u>social laws</u>. In the 1960s, for example, <u>homosexuality</u> became legal and <u>divorce</u> became easier.

3) However, <u>social attitudes</u> in Britain were quite <u>slow</u> to change. Families were still expected to have a '<u>nuclear</u>' structure — a mother, father and their children. Single-parent families, like Mrs Johnstone's, were <u>less common</u> than they are today, and were frowned upon by many.

4) Most families were <u>patriarchal</u> — this means the man led the family. He went to work, whilst the woman stayed at home to care for the children and household. This is the situation in the <u>Lyons</u> household. In contrast, Mrs Johnstone has to fill <u>both</u> roles after her husband walks out on her.

A magazine cover showing an 'ideal' family in the late 1950s

Britain in the Late Twentieth Century

When Russell was writing, Margaret Thatcher was Prime Minister

1) During the 1970s, Britain's <u>traditional industries</u> (such as coal mining and shipbuilding) were in <u>decline</u> because they were <u>inefficient</u> and struggling to keep up with <u>foreign competition</u>. Britain was suffering from a <u>recession</u>, and <u>unemployment</u> was rising.

2) <u>Margaret Thatcher</u> became Prime Minister in 1979. She believed that Britain's traditional industries weren't economically viable any more, and decided to <u>close them down</u>.

3) The decline of traditional industries in the 1970s and 1980s had a <u>huge impact</u> on working-class <u>communities</u>:

Many workers went on strike about the changes.

- There was <u>widespread unemployment</u> among the working classes.

- In many working-class communities, most men relied on a single industry for work. If that industry couldn't provide jobs, the <u>whole community</u> was left unemployed.

- Many people had to sign up for benefits (known as '<u>going on the dole</u>').

- Unemployment led to an increase in <u>depression</u> and <u>crime rates</u>.

Character — Mickey

Mickey <u>represents</u> the many working-class men who became unemployed in this period. He <u>loses</u> his job, signs onto the <u>dole</u> and despite three months of desperately searching for work, he can't find anything. This begins his descent into <u>depression</u>, and prompts him to turn to <u>crime</u>.

There was a strong class divide in Britain

1) Even before the industrial decline, there was a <u>sharp divide</u> in Britain between the working class and the middle class. The decline just made it <u>worse</u>.

2) Lots of working-class parents <u>struggled financially</u>, even if they were in work or on the dole. Many people found it difficult to afford even <u>basic things</u>, such as food, clothes and heating.

Character — Mr Lyons

Mr Lyons shows <u>no compassion</u> towards his secretary, Miss Jones, when he fires her. His own job as the factory manager is <u>secure</u>, so he simply dismisses her by saying "It's <u>just another sign / Of the times.</u>"

3) The <u>middle class</u> were <u>largely unaffected</u> by the industrial decline. Many of them didn't work in industry — they had jobs like teaching or accountancy instead. Those who did work in declining industries were <u>running them</u>, so they had transferable skills (like management) and could get <u>new jobs</u>.

4) There was also a class divide in <u>education</u>. Many middle-class parents could afford to send their children to <u>private school</u>. Often private school led to <u>university</u> and a <u>well-paid job</u> — as it does for Edward.

5) By <u>contrast</u>, for most working-class children (like the Johnstones), university <u>wasn't</u> an option. They needed to work when they left school to support their families, and they became <u>stuck</u> in the same <u>low-paid</u> jobs for life, with <u>little opportunity</u> to progress.

"...the same answer everywhere, nothin'..."

Reading these pages, you can kind of understand why Mickey loses his temper with Edward at Christmas. Edward thinks signing up for the dole would be easy because he's never experienced what it's really like.

Liverpool and Skelmersdale

Liverpool depended heavily on traditional industries, so it was <u>badly hit</u> by the industrial decline in the late twentieth century. The city's working-class areas were already pretty poor, and things went from bad to <u>worse</u>.

Liverpool suffered badly from the industrial decline

1) By the late twentieth century, Liverpool was a <u>major port</u> and had been a centre for trade for hundreds of years. This provided <u>lots of jobs</u> at the docks. Many jobs were also provided by the <u>shipbuilding</u> industry.

2) This made Liverpool <u>very vulnerable</u> to the industrial decline. In the early 1980s, Liverpool had one of the <u>highest unemployment rates</u> in the country.

3) Some men turned to <u>crime</u> and <u>gangs</u> in order to support themselves and their families. There were also <u>riots</u> in the early 1980s, fuelled by high levels of unemployment.

Character — Sammy

Sammy is involved in this <u>gang culture</u>. Whereas Mickey tries hard to find paid work, Sammy has been on the dole since he was sixteen. There's no mention of him <u>ever</u> having a job. Sammy seems to have <u>chosen</u> crime over employment.

Many Liverpool residents were rehoused in the twentieth century

1) After World War Two ended in 1945, Liverpool began rebuilding to replace the housing lost during bombing raids. Huge <u>new estates</u> of <u>council houses</u> were built (properties owned by the city council and rented to tenants).

2) However, lots of these new council houses were constructed so quickly and cheaply that they were <u>poor quality</u>. Most had no heating, indoor toilets or gardens. <u>Overcrowding</u> was a problem. This is the kind of housing that the Johnstones have in Act One.

3) In the 1960s, the government began building <u>New Towns</u>. These were small, existing towns, which were extended and redeveloped to provide more housing for nearby cities. <u>Skelmersdale</u> was one of these New Towns, and many people were moved from <u>Liverpool's</u> council estates to Skelmersdale.

An inspection of a Liverpool slum in 1962.

© Trinity Mirror / Mirrorpix / Alamy

4) Some residents were <u>upset</u> to be moved from the area they'd always known. Others saw it as an <u>opportunity</u> for a better life.

5) Skelmersdale was hit by the <u>same problems</u> as Liverpool when traditional industries went into decline. Many big employers <u>left</u> the town, so many <u>factory workers</u> lost their jobs.

Character — Mrs Johnstone

Mrs Johnstone is <u>overjoyed</u> when her family are rehoused in Skelmersdale, and has very <u>idealistic</u> ideas of what it will be like there.

As in most cities, Liverpool also has <u>wealthy areas</u>. Edward's house is described as "<u>big</u>" and "<u>up by the park</u>", to emphasise how its size and outdoor space are so <u>different</u> from the Johnstones' estate.

KEY QUOTE
"we'll be all right out here... away from the muck an' the dirt"
Mrs Johnstone gets a teeny bit carried away about moving to Skelmersdale. Before you know it, she's dancing round the streets and imagining having tea with the Pope. I hear he likes scones, Mrs J...

Practice Questions

These questions should help you get to grips with the past few pages. You only need to write a couple of words or sentences for the Quick Questions, but try to write about a paragraph for the In-depth ones.

Quick Questions

1) In which of these periods is *Blood Brothers* mostly set?
   a) 1930s-1950s
   b) 1960s-1980s
   c) 1970s-1990s

2) Explain in one sentence what is meant by the term 'youth culture'.

3) When *Blood Brothers* was written, what was the structure of most families in Britain?

4) a) Why were Britain's traditional industries in decline in the 1970s?
   b) Which Prime Minister decided that these industries weren't economically viable?

5) What does 'going on the dole' mean?

6) After losing their jobs, what did some men turn to support their families?

7) Give three of the common problems with council houses in Liverpool in the 1960s.

8) What is a 'New Town'?

In-depth Questions

1) Look again at the way Mr Lyons' sacking of Miss Jones is presented.
   What might this suggest about Russell's own attitudes to social class?

2) Pick a passage from the play which shows what life was like for working-class families in Britain in the late twentieth century. How do you think it shows this?

3) How were educational opportunities different for working-class and middle-class people in the late twentieth century? Why is this important in the play?

4) Explain some of the advantages and disadvantages of the New Towns programme in the 1960s.
   How are these advantages and disadvantages relevant to the play?

Analysis of Act One — The Scene is Set

So it's time to get stuck in to the juicy details. You need to know the play inside out and back to front for the exam, so if you're still a little shaky on the plot, have another look over the summary on pages 4-5.

The play begins with the ending

1) The Narrator's opening speech tells the basic story of the play. His speech takes the form of a prologue (see p.44).

2) This means the audience knows how the story ends before it even begins, which suggests the characters can't escape fate.

3) The Narrator speaks in rhyme and uses old-fashioned and mystical phrases like "Of one womb born" and "lie slain". This creates an unsettling and ominous atmosphere.

Theme — Fate and Superstition

The link between the Narrator and Fate is established straightaway — every time he reappears, it reminds us that the twins are going to die.

Mrs Johnstone sings about her past

1) Mrs Johnstone's story makes the audience feel sympathy for her — her husband has "walked out" on her, leaving her with seven children to look after and another on the way.

2) Mrs Johnstone introduces the motifs of Marilyn Monroe and dancing (see p.49):

A motif is a recurring symbol.

- At this point, Marilyn Monroe is used to represent perfection and a glamorous lifestyle.

- Dancing symbolises freedom and happiness. Marriage and children take that away from Mrs Johnstone.

3) The Milkman interrupts her and her children start complaining. She can't even dream about happiness because her real-life problems get in the way.

Writer's Techniques

The children are all offstage as they shout their complaints, whilst Mrs Johnstone "*stands alone*". This emphasises that Mrs Johnstone is surrounded by overwhelming responsibility, which she has to deal with on her own.

The class divide is obvious from the start

1) Mrs Johnstone arrives at Mrs Lyons' house with "*a brush, dusters and a mop bucket*", whereas Mrs Lyons is carrying a parcel containing new shoes.

2) Some key differences are immediately established:

- Mrs Johnstone is poor, whereas Mrs Lyons is rich.
- Mrs Johnstone works, whereas Mrs Lyons spends the money that her husband earns.
- Mrs Johnstone "can't stop" having children, whereas Mrs Lyons "can't have kids".
- Mrs Johnstone is superstitious, whereas Mrs Lyons is not.

Write about how Russell establishes some key themes...

Right from the off, Russell puts social class at the forefront of the audience's minds — it's clear that the two families are very different. The prologue also establishes the twins' fate. Bit of a spoiler, really...

Analysis of Act One — The Agreement

So Mrs J is having twins... The logical thing to do is to give one to that woman whose house you've just started cleaning — it is a lovely house after all. What could possibly go wrong?

There are twins on the way

1) When Mrs Johnstone finds out she's expecting twins, she is *"numbed by the news"*. Her <u>shock</u> makes her <u>vulnerable</u> when Mrs Lyons tells her to "Give one to me."

2) Mrs Lyons doesn't show any <u>sympathy</u> for Mrs Johnstone's <u>situation</u>. She puts a cushion up her dress and plans what she'll tell her husband <u>before</u> Mrs Johnstone has even agreed.

© Donald Cooper/Photostage.co.uk

3) Mrs Lyons then <u>pressures</u> Mrs Johnstone to agree:

- She <u>interrupts</u> her as she says "y' can't just...", and doesn't give her a chance to <u>think</u> or <u>refuse</u>.
- She uses <u>imperatives</u> such as "<u>tell me</u>" and "<u>Look, look</u>" — she <u>controls</u> the conversation.
- She makes <u>promises</u> about the life she'll give the child, such as "He'd have all his own toys".
- She tells Mrs Johnstone that she can <u>see</u> the child every day.
- She "*nods enthusiastically*" in order to <u>influence</u> Mrs Johnstone's decision.
- She <u>twists</u> what Mrs Johnstone has told her and uses it to <u>play</u> on her <u>fears</u>, asking "how can you possibly avoid some of them being put into care?"

4) Mrs Johnstone only <u>nods</u> her agreement — this shows that she's <u>reluctant</u> but feels that she has no choice.

5) Mrs Lyons <u>immediately</u> puts the plan into action — she doesn't give Mrs Johnstone the chance to <u>think</u> about her decision.

> **Writer's Techniques**
>
> The Narrator refers to a "thought <u>conceived</u>" and a "deal... <u>born</u>", linking the <u>plan</u> to <u>pregnancy</u>.

Mrs Lyons takes Edward

1) When the time comes to give one of the twins up, Mrs Johnstone is <u>reluctant</u>, telling Mrs Lyons that "they're a pair, they go together", but Mrs Lyons plays on her <u>superstitious nature</u> by reminding her that she "swore on the Bible".

> **Writer's Techniques — Structure**
>
> <u>Debt collectors</u> are waiting for Mrs Johnstone when she gets home from the hospital. This highlights the <u>parallels</u> between her <u>financial debt</u> and her <u>pregnancy</u> — she <u>can't afford</u> to keep her <u>belongings</u>, just as she can't afford to keep both <u>twins</u>.

> **Theme — Money and Social Class**
>
> <u>Money</u> gives Mrs Lyons <u>power</u> — it allows her to employ and sack Mrs Johnstone. Her <u>class</u> also gives her <u>leverage</u> — she knows that if the matter went to the police, they would believe her over Mrs Johnstone.

2) Later, Mrs Lyons's <u>paranoia</u> begins to grow when she sees Mrs Johnstone "fussing over the baby" — this is the start of her deep-seated <u>insecurity</u> about her relationship with Edward. She thinks she can solve the problem by <u>sacking</u> Mrs Johnstone.

3) Mrs Lyons <u>invents</u> the superstition that the twins will <u>die</u> "if either twin learns that he was once a pair". She wants to <u>scare</u> Mrs Johnstone into never telling the boys the truth.

"kids can't live on love alone."

You're not wrong there, Mrs J. The Narrator's already had a pop at her, saying she has a heart of stone, but really she knows that she <u>can't afford</u> to look after both twins. She's just doing what she thinks is best.

Analysis of Act One — The Twins Meet

Seven years have gone by and the twins are now... you guessed it, seven. Mickey has pretty normal interests — worms, swearing, weeing through letterboxes — and he introduces Edward to this magical new world.

Mickey and Edward meet and become blood brothers

KEY SCENE

1) Mrs Johnstone and Mrs Lyons both try to <u>stop</u> the boys from <u>meeting</u> — they're "not allowed" to play near one another's houses. Both boys <u>disobey</u> their mothers.

Theme — Fate

The boys meet despite their mothers' efforts to keep them apart. This shows the <u>inevitability</u> of their friendship.

2) The boys' <u>language</u> highlights the <u>difference</u> in their social class. Mickey's language is full of <u>slang</u> and <u>swear words</u> like "bleedin'" and "pissed off". Edward uses <u>middle-class</u> words like "super" and "smashing".

3) They immediately decide to be best friends and then "blood brothers". This is <u>dramatic irony</u> — the audience knows that they're brothers, but the characters don't.

The children's game foreshadows later events

1) Mickey, Sammy, Linda and other children play a <u>game</u> of "*goodies and baddies*". <u>Edward</u> stands "*watching*" them, which shows his <u>longing</u> to be part of their world.

2) The game is <u>lighthearted</u> — it "doesn't matter" if you die. This highlights the <u>innocence</u> of childhood (p.38). But there are also <u>darker</u> undertones — the <u>violence</u> of the game <u>foreshadows</u> the robbery (see p.16), and Mickey and Edward's deaths.

Foreshadowing is when the writer hints at a future event.

3) <u>Linda</u> "*moves in to <u>protect</u> Mickey*" when the others pick on him. This establishes her <u>loyalty</u> to Mickey — she looks after and stands by him, as she will <u>throughout</u> the play (see p.28).

4) <u>Sammy</u> leads the bullying of his brother. This shows that he has a <u>cruel</u> nature and <u>no loyalty</u> to Mickey.

Mrs Lyons is growing more paranoid

1) Mrs Lyons knows that there is a <u>connection</u> between Edward and the Johnstones, and it worries her:

- Edward has picked up <u>bad language</u> from Mickey, and Mrs Lyons reacts <u>furiously</u> — she's <u>scared</u> that he is becoming more like the Johnstones.

- She tries to <u>deny</u> the connection, telling Edward "You are my son, mine".

Character — Mrs Lyons

Earlier in the play, Mrs Lyons' reasoning was <u>clear</u>. Now, her attempts to <u>persuade</u> her husband are based on <u>irrational feelings</u>. This suggests she's losing her grip on <u>reality</u>.

2) There are hints that Mrs Lyons is starting to <u>believe</u> the <u>superstition</u> she made up about separated twins. When Edward goes off with Mickey and Linda, she tries desperately to persuade her husband that they should move away, telling him "if we stay here I feel that something terrible will happen".

3) She also dramatically "*sweeps*" a pair of <u>shoes</u> off the table, which echoes Mrs Johnstone's earlier uneasiness. Her growing belief in superstition is making her <u>increasingly unstable</u>.

KEY QUOTE

"I will always defend my brother."

That's quite a promise to make to some kid you just met. In all fairness to them, they stick to it for a while, but thanks to the Narrator's spoiler earlier on, we know that things aren't always going to stay this peachy...

Analysis of Act One — Both Families Move Away

Poor Edward — just when he finds a shiny new best mate, said mate gets him into trouble with the police. It all proves too much for the Lyonses, who make like a tree and leave. I'll get my coat.

The policeman treats the two families very differently

1) Edward <u>sneaks out</u> to play with Mickey and Linda, and the three of them are caught misbehaving by a <u>policeman</u>.

2) The policeman's reactions show how the characters are treated <u>differently</u>, depending on their social class:

Theme — Identity

The policeman is harder on Mickey because of Sammy's <u>reputation</u>. This shows how hard it is to <u>escape</u> prejudice based on <u>upbringing</u>.

- He <u>swears</u> at Mrs Johnstone, telling her "there'll be no more bloody warnings", and he <u>threatens</u> her with court. He also <u>patronises</u> her, asking her "do you understand that?"
- He is <u>polite</u> and <u>subservient</u> to Mr Lyons, advising him not to let Edward "mix with the likes of them". He removes his helmet — a <u>symbol</u> of his authority — which makes him seem less <u>imposing</u>.

The Lyonses decide to move away

1) Although Mr Lyons initially <u>ignored</u> his wife's desire to move, the encounter with the policeman <u>persuades</u> him (see p.41).

2) Edward gets <u>upset</u> about moving and Mrs Johnstone "*Cradles him, letting him cry*" — this is a very <u>maternal image</u> and suggests that she still thinks of him as her son.

3) Mrs Johnstone gives Edward a <u>locket</u> — this creates a <u>bond</u> with him and ensures he won't <u>forget</u> the Johnstones.

Writer's Techniques — 'Blood Brothers' on the Stage

When the Lyonses are moving, they are on "*their side of the stage*" — this represents the <u>geographical and social distance</u> between the two families. When Edward speaks the word "Goodbye", he's trying to <u>cross</u> this divide.

The Johnstones find out they're being moved

KEY SCENE

1) Despite the <u>distance</u> between the boys, the <u>bond</u> between them is clear:

- Edward picks up Mickey's <u>superstitions</u>, e.g. "*covering his eyes*" when he sees a magpie.
- They sing 'My Friend' together, using the same melody and pattern of lyrics.

2) The Johnstones find out they're <u>being moved</u> to Skelmersdale (see p.8). Mrs Johnstone sees this as a chance to "begin again".

Theme — Identity

Mrs Johnstone is <u>eager</u> to move and <u>escape</u> her reputation.

3) When they arrive, Mrs Johnstone <u>immediately</u> has to <u>tell Sammy</u> to "Get off that bleedin' cow". This suggests that not everything will be fixed by their move.

EXAM TIP

Write about how different social classes are treated...

The policeman's visit in this section is very important, because it shows how the different classes are treated by the authorities in the play. This highlights Willy Russell's message about class inequality.

Analysis of Act Two — Skelmersdale

Time moves on between the acts. Whilst the audience spend the interval scoffing ice cream in the foyer, the twins age rapidly, and have reached the ripe old age of fourteen by the time everyone retakes their seats.

Life seems better in Skelmersdale, but it's far from perfect

1) In Skelmersdale, Mrs Johnstone seems <u>happy</u> and <u>free</u>:

- She can pay her "bills <u>on time</u>".
- The milkman takes her "<u>dancing</u>" and compares her to "<u>Marilyn Monroe</u>".

2) However, Sammy <u>burns</u> the school down and then <u>robs</u> the bus conductor at knife point — his behaviour has become <u>criminal</u>.

Writer's Techniques — Motifs

Mrs Johnstone hopes Edward is "OK, / Not like Marilyn Monroe". This is the first <u>negative</u> reference to Marilyn Monroe. It's <u>ominous</u> because it suggests that even if something seems <u>perfect</u>, it may not stay that way.

Theme — Fate

The Narrator (as the Conductor) says "No one gets off without the price bein' paid", which reminds us of the twins' <u>fate</u>.

1) Mrs Lyons and Edward are also <u>dancing</u> — this suggests that they are happy on the <u>surface</u>.

2) However, Edward is "*very awkward*" and complains that "we hardly ever see a girl", suggesting that he's <u>not very happy</u>.

3) Despite moving away, Mrs Lyons is still <u>paranoid</u>:

- She says "We have had a very good time this holiday, though, haven't we?", highlighting her <u>insecurity</u> and <u>desperate</u> need for Edward's approval.
- She also asks him "We're safe here, aren't we?" — her question implies that she still doesn't feel <u>free</u> of the Johnstones.

The boys' schools highlight the differences in their upbringing

1) Edward's <u>private school</u> is <u>strict</u> and <u>formal</u> — his teacher threatens to have him "flogged" and Edward calls him "<u>sir</u>".

2) Mickey's <u>state school</u> is "*all <u>boredom</u> and <u>futility</u>*" and far <u>less formal</u> — the teacher calls a pupil a "borin' little turd".

Writer's Techniques

Willy Russell <u>juxtaposes</u> the school scenes to <u>highlight</u> the <u>differences</u> between them.

Juxtaposing means putting two things next to one another to contrast them.

Character — Linda

In Mickey's school scene, Linda <u>sticks up</u> for him and tells him she <u>loves</u> him. This hints at their later <u>relationship</u>.

3) The boys are both suspended for <u>rebelling</u> against authority. This suggests that despite their different upbringings, there are <u>similarities</u> between them.

Write about how Russell uses the school scenes...

It's no mistake that Russell starts Act Two with <u>both</u> twins' school lives. It's a dramatic technique that highlights the similarities in their personalities, and the differences in their educational opportunities. Nifty.

Analysis of Act Two — The Twins Meet Again

A lot happens in this bit of the play — the boys meet, Mrs Lyons goes mad(der) and we see the twins grow up. Time flies when you're using a dramatic device to show several years passing in a few minutes.

The boys renew their friendship

Writer's Techniques

The song 'That Guy' has the same melody as 'My Child', hinting at the link between Edward and the Johnstones.

1) Back in Skelmersdale, the boys see each other in the distance. They sing about how they want to look like the other, both saying "Each part of his face / Is in just the right place" — this highlights their teenage insecurity and adds humour since they're actually twins.

2) Mickey's "Gis a ciggie" mirrors his "Gis a sweet" from their first meeting — they act the same around each other as they used to.

3) Mickey knows what Edward is saying even when he doesn't finish his sentences. For example, when Edward says "I only live...", Mickey replies "I know", showing that they're still connected.

4) Their rapid dialogue reveals their excitement at being reunited.

Character — Edward

Edward describes Mrs Johnstone as "fabulous" — she represents a freedom from the rules and paranoia of Mrs Lyons.

Mrs Lyons realises she hasn't escaped the Johnstones

1) Mrs Lyons sees the boys together, which renews her panic about Edward's connection to the Johnstones. She confronts Mrs Johnstone, telling her that "I took him. But I never made him mine."

2) Mrs Lyons is paranoid that Mrs Johnstone is following her — Mrs Johnstone explains that they were simply "rehoused here". This highlights how fate has brought the twins together again.

3) Mrs Lyons tries to bribe Mrs Johnstone to leave Skelmersdale. When this fails, she attacks Mrs Johnstone with a knife, showing her growing insanity. Her madness is emphasised by her growing belief in superstition, culminating in her shouting "I curse you. Witch!" at Mrs Johnstone.

Mickey, Edward and Linda grow up

1) The twins and Linda become inseparable — this is highlighted by the montage which shows them ageing from fourteen to eighteen at *"the fairground"*, *"the chip shop"* and *"the beach"*. The stage directions mention that all three of them smile a lot, which emphasises the joy and freedom of youth.

Writer's Techniques — Structure

Russell uses the montage (see p.44) as a dramatic technique to move the play forwards, but the speed at which the time passes on stage may also symbolise the fleetingness of youth.

2) However, there are darker undertones as the Narrator likens them to "lambs in spring" being raised for slaughter — this is a reminder that their happiness won't last.

3) After convincing Mickey to ask Linda out, Edward leaves for university, symbolising the end of childhood.

KEY QUOTE

"They care not for what's at the end of the day."

And given what *is* at the end of the day, perhaps it's better if they don't give it too much thought. Being chased by llamas and falling in a cesspit isn't a fate anyone would choose. Oops, did I give the ending away?

Analysis of Act Two — The Twins Drift Apart
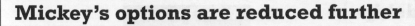

Now the boys are adults, cracks develop in their friendship. It's so sad — I'm off to look at my photo of skateboarding rabbits, it's the only thing that'll cheer me up. Oh, alright, here you go:

Mickey's options are reduced further

1) Linda falls <u>pregnant</u> by Mickey and they marry. Having an <u>unplanned child</u> at a <u>young age</u> mirrors Mrs Johnstone's life.

2) Mickey is made <u>redundant</u> — Mr Lyons represents <u>unsympathetic</u>, <u>middle-class</u> bosses whose jobs are <u>safe</u>.

3) Mickey's redundancy and the song 'Miss Jones' symbolise the <u>decline</u> of Britain's traditional industries and the <u>impact</u> this had on the working classes.

4) During the song, the stage is full of people in the same situation. This highlights the <u>widespread unemployment</u> and <u>reliance</u> on the <u>dole</u> (see p.7).

© Donald Cooper/Photostage.co.uk

Edward and Mickey's differences become more pronounced

1) Edward is at university, and living the life that Mrs Johnstone hoped he would. His middle-class <u>privilege</u> stands out against the <u>backdrop</u> of mass working-class unemployment.

2) Edward <u>doesn't see</u> why having a job is "so important" to Mickey and offers him money. He has no understanding of Mickey's need to be <u>independent</u>.

3) The twins argue for the first time. The <u>differences</u> they <u>admired</u> as children are now driving them apart.

> **Theme — Childhood and Growing Up**
>
> Mickey is facing the <u>harsh realities</u> of adult life. He thinks that Edward is "still a kid" who doesn't "need to" grow up because he can rely on his <u>parents' money</u> and status.

Mickey's desperation leads him to crime

KEY SCENE

1) While Sammy persuades Mickey to help with a <u>robbery</u>, Edward asks Linda to <u>marry</u> him. He doesn't know that Linda has already married Mickey, which emphasises the <u>distance</u> between the boys.

2) By showing the two conversations <u>simultaneously</u>, Russell increases the <u>pace</u> of the scene. It also emphasises that both boys are at a <u>crossroads</u> — Mickey has to choose whether to commit a crime and Edward whether to try to take his best friend's wife. Both make the <u>wrong choice</u>.

> **Writer's Techniques — Language**
>
> After the robbery, Mickey repeats "You shot him, you shot him" and Sammy replies "I know I bloody did." This, together with the <u>rhyme</u> of "did" and "hid", <u>mirrors</u> the pattern of speech in the <u>children's game</u> in Act One. This emphasises that their childhood is <u>over</u> and it's not "just a game" anymore.

3) During his time in jail, Mickey becomes <u>depressed</u> and <u>hooked</u> on anti-depressants. Mrs Johnstone likens Mickey's problems to those of Marilyn Monroe and says that "His mind's gone dancing". The <u>motifs</u> of Monroe and dancing were used previously to symbolise <u>happiness</u>. Now, they emphasise how wrong things have gone for Mickey.

KEY QUOTE

"you've not had much of a life with me, have y'?"

That's what I said to my pet satsuma, Monty, just before I ate him. It was true — he'd been sitting in that fruit bowl for nearly a week, watching his friends get picked off one by one. Yep, life is tough if you're a citrus fruit.

Analysis of Act Two — The Twins Die

So here we have it, the ending that we all knew was coming. Willy Russell builds the tension on stage and even though we knew it was going to happen, it still comes as a bit of a shock...

Mickey's behaviour pushes Linda towards Edward

1) Mickey gets out of jail but he is still <u>depressed</u> and on <u>pills</u>. He has already pushed Edward away and he starts to do the same to Linda, telling her to "leave me alone".

2) Linda gets Mickey a job and a house for them both thanks to "some feller" — the audience (and Mickey) know it's Edward, and her refusal to admit this suggests that she feels <u>guilty</u>.

3) The Narrator says that "There's a girl inside the woman", hinting that Linda is longing for the <u>freedom</u> of her <u>childhood</u>. Edward represents this <u>freedom</u>, and Linda is drawn to him because of the stresses of her adult life.

The pace of the action builds up

1) In an effort to drive the twins <u>apart</u>, Mrs Lyons shows Mickey that Edward and Linda are together.

Character — Mrs Lyons

This is the <u>first time</u> we've seen Mrs Lyons since she tried to attack Mrs Johnstone. She has <u>no lines</u>, which makes her seem like an empty shell of her former self.

2) The sense of <u>panic</u> builds — Mickey is "*breaking through groups of people*" as Mrs Johnstone "*frantically*" chases him, "*screaming*" his name.

3) The Narrator says "the devil's got your number" throughout the play as a <u>reminder</u> of what's to come, but now "he's callin' your number up today" — the characters are soon going to <u>meet their fate</u>. His speech culminates with the lines "Today / Today / TODAY!" — everything has been <u>building up</u> to this moment.

Events reach their inevitable conclusion

1) Armed with Sammy's <u>gun</u>, Mickey interrupts Edward during a speech.

2) Mrs Johnstone finally <u>reveals</u> the truth, and Mickey exclaims "I could have been him!". Mickey clearly believes that <u>identity</u> is determined by <u>upbringing</u> (see p.40).

Writer's Techniques

<u>Guns</u> feature throughout the play (see p.49), <u>foreshadowing</u> the ending.

3) Mickey shoots Edward by <u>accident</u> — the gun "*explodes*" as he "*waves*" it, and the policemen shoot him in response. Both deaths occur very quickly, with no speech, highlighting how <u>senseless</u> they are.

- The Narrator asks whether the twins' deaths were due to <u>superstition</u> or <u>class</u> — he raises the question of whether the tragedy could have been <u>avoided</u> if it weren't for <u>class divides</u> (see p.37).

- The Narrator and Mrs Johnstone <u>repeat</u> lines from the prologue — this makes the play <u>cyclical</u> (see p.44), hinting at the way people <u>can't escape</u> the effect that social class has on their lives.

 ## "Why didn't you give me away?"

Mickey thinks that he'd have turned out just like Edward if he'd been given away — whether or not that's true is up for debate. The twins have finally met their fate and we're left to question why it happened.

Practice Questions

It's time to test how much you know about 'Blood Brothers' with these shiny, new, made-to-measure questions. You only need to write a few words to answer each one, so you should whip through these like a cheetah wearing roller skates. Assuming said cheetah knew how to use roller skates. And was on a relatively hard, smooth surface. You get the idea. Now get answering...

Quick Questions

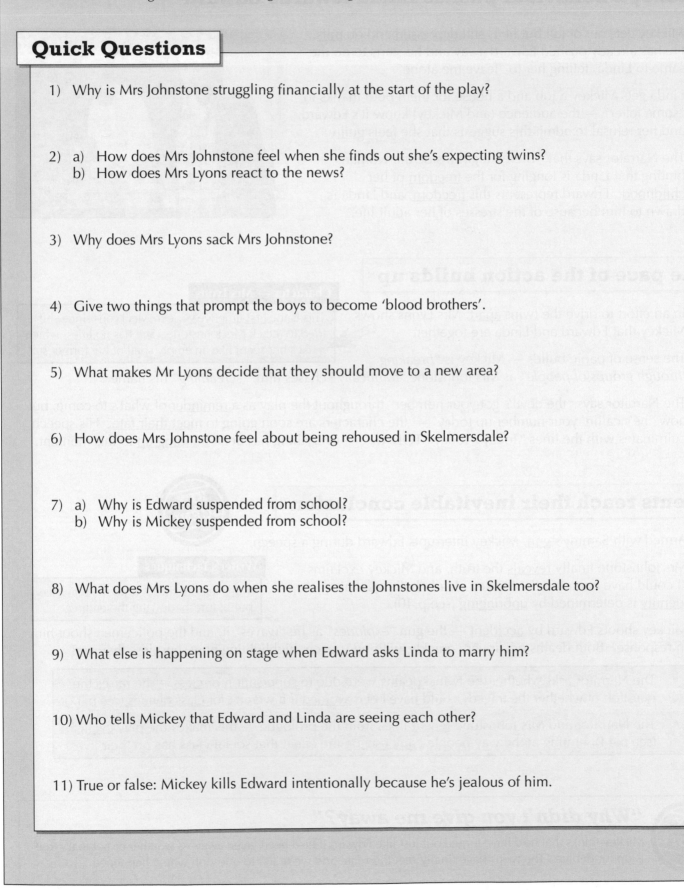

1) Why is Mrs Johnstone struggling financially at the start of the play?

2) a) How does Mrs Johnstone feel when she finds out she's expecting twins?
   b) How does Mrs Lyons react to the news?

3) Why does Mrs Lyons sack Mrs Johnstone?

4) Give two things that prompt the boys to become 'blood brothers'.

5) What makes Mr Lyons decide that they should move to a new area?

6) How does Mrs Johnstone feel about being rehoused in Skelmersdale?

7) a) Why is Edward suspended from school?
   b) Why is Mickey suspended from school?

8) What does Mrs Lyons do when she realises the Johnstones live in Skelmersdale too?

9) What else is happening on stage when Edward asks Linda to marry him?

10) Who tells Mickey that Edward and Linda are seeing each other?

11) True or false: Mickey kills Edward intentionally because he's jealous of him.

Practice Questions

These questions are a little bit trickier than the ones on the previous page, but if you've been paying attention they shouldn't cause you too many problems. Try to write a paragraph or two for each one — I promise you it'll be worth it come exam day. When you've finished, I give you leave to go and do an hour's wholesome activity (kite-flying, badger-hugging or similar) before you move on to Section Three.

In-depth Questions

1) How does Willy Russell use Mrs Johnstone's first conversation with Mrs Lyons to establish the class divide between the two families?

2) To what extent is Mrs Lyons' later madness hinted at from the start of the play?

3) Look again at Mickey and Edward's first meeting. What are your initial impressions of Mickey and Edward from this scene?

4) Reread the policeman's visits to the two families. Why do you think Russell chose to include these visits in the play?

5) How does the relationship between Mr and Mrs Lyons change during the course of Act One? How does it stay the same?

6) What hints are there throughout the play that the twins share a bond deeper than friendship?

7) Do you think that life is better for the Johnstones in Skelmersdale than it was in Liverpool? Explain your answer.

8) How and why is Mickey's life different from Edward's when Edward first returns from university?

9) How and why does Russell emphasise the senseless nature of the twins' deaths?

Character Profile — Mrs Johnstone

For the exam, you'll need to know the play's characters better than you know your best mates, so this section is important. After you've read about a character, try closing the book and jotting down their <u>key points</u>.

Mrs Johnstone is trapped by poverty

1) Mrs Johnstone is <u>very poor</u>. She struggles to provide for her many children.

2) This has made her <u>old</u> before her time — she's *"aged thirty but looks more like fifty."*

3) Mrs Johnstone's poverty means that she <u>lacks control</u> over her life:

Mrs Johnstone is...

- **poor** — "If I'm careful we can just scrape by"
- **superstitious** — "never put new shoes on a table"
- **loving** — *"She takes him. Cradles him, letting him cry."*
- **optimistic** — "'Ey, we'll be all right out here, son"

- When she became pregnant, she had <u>no choice</u> but to marry Mr Johnstone. This made her <u>financially dependent</u> on a man who then walked out on her.

- Mrs Lyons <u>manipulates</u> her into giving up Edward. Mrs Johnstone is <u>persuaded</u> by the idea of a <u>better life</u> for her son, and the <u>false promise</u> that she can see him every day.

- Mrs Johnstone is <u>rehoused</u> by the council, and told about this in a <u>letter</u>. She has <u>no say</u> in the matter.

Britain in the Late Twentieth Century

Sex before marriage was <u>not</u> socially acceptable. If an unmarried woman became pregnant, the father was expected to marry her <u>quickly</u>.

Theme — Money and Social Class

Mrs Johnstone is <u>forced</u> into this decision by lack of <u>money</u>. She can't afford to keep both twins.

4) Mrs Johnstone is also <u>impressionable</u>. For example, her husband gave her "<u>the chat</u>" when they met, suggesting that she <u>fell</u> for his charms. The fact that she's easily influenced makes her <u>vulnerable</u>.

5) She also makes some <u>irresponsible</u> decisions. She orders things from catalogues because it feels like "years" until you have to pay for them, but they're <u>repossessed</u> because she can't afford them.

She is superstitious, which makes her vulnerable

1) Mrs Johnstone's superstitious belief has a <u>big impact</u> on her life.

2) Most importantly, superstition <u>separates</u> her from Edward. She instantly believes the superstition Mrs Lyons invents — that the boys will die if they ever find out they're twins. This <u>stops her</u> from taking Edward back or telling anyone, which gives Mrs Lyons <u>power over her</u>.

3) Superstitions also make Mrs Johnstone <u>feel vulnerable</u>. She says "you never know what'll happen" if you put new shoes on the table, showing that she <u>worries</u> about the <u>consequences</u> of ignoring superstitions.

Writer's Techniques — Language

Mrs Johnstone's language is <u>frantic</u> when she sees the shoes on the table. She <u>tells</u> Mrs Lyons to "take them off", which is out of character. <u>Ellipses</u> show that she is panicking — "The shoes... the shoes..." She is genuinely <u>frightened</u> of what will happen.

© Nils Jorgensen/REX

There are hints that Mrs Johnstone is <u>Catholic</u>, such as her fear of the "devil" and picture of the Pope. She tells Mrs Lyons that she wants to keep both twins, but gives in when Mrs Lyons reminds her that she "swore on the <u>Bible</u>". Religious belief is <u>another</u> thing that keeps Mrs Johnstone under Mrs Lyons' control.

Character Profile — Mrs Johnstone

She's compassionate, but she struggles to control her children

1) Mrs Johnstone is <u>openly loving</u> towards her <u>children</u>, and she <u>understands</u> them.

Openly loving

- Talking about her children, she tells Mrs Lyons " I <u>love the bones</u> of every one of them."
- She is <u>physically</u> affectionate. She "*cradles*" Edward and often <u>hugs</u> and <u>kisses</u> Mickey.

Understanding

- She <u>forgives</u> her children for their wrongdoing, for example saying that Sammy burning his school down is "very easily done".
- She guesses which film the twins want to see, and lets them, saying she wasn't "born yesterday". This shows that she's <u>broad-minded</u> and <u>non-judgemental</u>.
- She also understands her children's <u>feelings</u>. For example, she knows about Mickey's feelings for Linda from age fourteen. She also <u>narrates</u> Edward and Linda's affair, suggesting that she <u>empathises</u> with them.

© Nils Jorgensen/REX

2) However, Mrs Johnstone's children are also <u>out of control</u>. She's "threatened by the welfare people", who want to put some of them into <u>care</u>, and Sammy's behaviour becomes steadily <u>worse</u> (see p.29). Her forgiving approach may not always be <u>appropriate</u>.

Character — Mrs Lyons

Mrs Johnstone's approach to mothering <u>contrasts</u> strongly with Mrs Lyons, who is much stricter with Edward but not as understanding (see p.22).

Mrs Johnstone is optimistic despite the problems she faces

1) Despite her <u>tough</u> situation, Mrs Johnstone <u>remains hopeful</u>. This makes her a more <u>sympathetic</u> character.

2) She dreams of a <u>better life</u> for herself and her children. This is her key motivation in giving <u>Edward</u> away — with Mrs Lyons, he "wouldn't have to worry where / His next meal was comin' from."

3) Her positivity is also shown in her attitude to <u>Skelmersdale</u> — she thinks she can "<u>begin again</u>" there, and leave behind her <u>bad reputation</u>.

4) Even when Skelmersdale <u>isn't</u> all she'd hoped for, Mrs Johnstone stays <u>optimistic</u>. The neighbours sometimes fight, but she focuses on how it's "never in the week". She always tries to make the <u>best</u> of her situation.

5) Mrs Johnstone's optimism makes the ending of the play more <u>tragic</u>. In the final song, she refers to the twins' deaths as a "story", a "dream", a "show" and a "game", as if she <u>can't accept</u> what's happened.

Writer's Techniques — Motifs

<u>Marilyn Monroe</u> initially represents Mrs Johnstone's happiness and her dreams of a better life. The mention of Monroe in the final song shows how Mrs Johnstone's hopes have come to <u>nothing</u>.

EXAM TIP

Write about Mrs Johnstone's attitude to her problems...

In the prologue, the Narrator describes Mrs Johnstone as a "mother, so cruel", but in the rest of the play she's presented as a sympathetic character, who always wants the best for her children. Yeah, back off, Narrator.

Character Profile — Mr and Mrs Lyons

The Lyonses — middle-class, wealthy, a beautiful home and a well-mannered son. Paradise? Not quite...

The Lyonses are wealthy but unhappy

1) The Lyonses are a <u>typical</u> late-twentieth-century middle-class couple. They have plenty of <u>money</u>, which Mr Lyons <u>earns</u>, whilst Mrs Lyons stays at <u>home</u> (and spends her husband's wages).

2) Mrs Lyons is <u>desperate</u> for a child — her "rather large" house emphasises how <u>empty</u> her life feels without children. She thought children would just "<u>come along</u>", which makes her childlessness more painful.

> **Theme — Gender**
>
> In the 1960s and 70s, women were <u>expected</u> to have children. Mrs Lyons has none, so she feels she's <u>failed</u> as a <u>woman</u> (see p.41).

3) Her desperation makes her very <u>idealistic</u>. She's "<u>dreamed</u>" of all the things she'd do with her son, and she paints a romantic picture of the "games we'd play" and the "jokes we'd share".

4) In <u>reality</u>, Mrs Lyons finds motherhood difficult. For example, she seeks <u>reassurance</u> from Edward that they've "had a very good time" in the holidays. This shows she's <u>insecure</u> about her mothering abilities and relationship with Edward.

© Donald Cooper/Photostage.co.uk

5) She <u>smothers</u> Edward, and doesn't want him "out playing" with other children. This shows that she's <u>over-protective</u>.

> Many of Mrs Lyons' insecurities are caused by the fact that Edward <u>isn't hers</u>. This makes her increasingly paranoid (p.23).

Mrs Lyons is...

- **desperate for a child** — "We've been trying for such a long time now..."
- **manipulative** — "you'd be able to see him every day"
- **paranoid** — "I feel that something terrible will happen"

Mr Lyons is...

- **work-driven** — "I've got a board meeting. I really must dash."
- **unsympathetic** — "It's just another sign / Of the times"

Mrs Lyons is very manipulative

1) Mrs Lyons <u>exploits</u> Mrs Johnstone's poverty to persuade her to give up a child. She uses <u>rhetorical questions</u>, such as "how can you possibly avoid some of them being put into care?", to make her argument sound <u>reasonable</u> and <u>persuasive</u>.

2) She also exploits Mrs Johnstone's superstitious belief, by making up a superstition to stop her telling anyone about the boys — she uses other people's <u>weaknesses</u> to her <u>advantage</u>.

3) Once she's got Edward, she fires Mrs Johnstone to stop her bonding with him. This shows that she's <u>not interested</u> in other people's problems and is prepared to <u>hurt</u> them to get what she wants.

4) Mrs Lyons <u>lies</u> to her husband throughout the play. He "wanted his own son, not someone else's", but she adopts a child <u>behind his back</u>. After Edward is born, she uses Mr Lyons' <u>lack of knowledge</u> about "things to buy for the baby" to get the cash to pay off Mrs Johnstone.

5) She reveals Edward and Linda's affair to Mickey because it <u>suits her</u> for the twins to fall out — she puts her own agenda <u>before</u> Edward's happiness.

> **Theme — Fate and Superstition**
>
> Mrs Lyons <u>takes action</u> to try to <u>change fate</u> — see p.36.

Character Profile — Mr and Mrs Lyons

Mrs Lyons changes in the course of the play

1) At the start of the play, Mrs Lyons is <u>in control</u>. She <u>dominates</u> Mrs Johnstone, and gets what she wants.

<u>Commands</u> like "<u>they shall</u> be raised apart" and "<u>you won't</u> tell anyone" establish her authority.

2) Mrs Lyons struggles to control her <u>anger</u> when Edward swears, hitting him *"hard and instinctively"*.

Afterwards, she <u>repeats phrases</u> such as "my son", showing her panic that she's pushed him away.

3) She becomes <u>paranoid</u> about Edward's relationship with the Johnstones, and wants to move away.

<u>Repetition</u> and <u>ellipses</u> show that she's obsessive, and is losing her ability to argue properly — "It's just...it's these people...these people..."

4) Mrs Lyons is driven <u>mad</u> by her fear, and tries to stab Mrs Johnstone with a kitchen knife.

Her language is <u>frantic</u>. She <u>exclaims</u> that Mrs Johnstone is a "Witch!" and curses her.

- The chant about the "mad woman" adds to the <u>tension</u> of this scene. It's spoken from <u>off-stage</u>, as if it's a chorus of voices in Mrs Lyons' head, and the <u>repetition</u> adds to the frantic atmosphere.

- The warning that you won't "grow any further" if she looks at you also suggests she's a <u>threat</u> to children (see p.45), which shows how her dreams of motherhood have <u>fallen apart</u>.

5) Mrs Lyons initially believes that "an adopted child can become <u>one's own</u>", but she's constantly worried about the Johnstones "<u>drawing</u>" Edward away. She ends up saying "I never made him <u>mine</u>" — she feels she never managed to change his <u>natural identity</u> (see p.40).

Theme — Superstition

As Mrs Lyons loses control of her life and her emotions, she also starts to believe in <u>superstitions</u>. She *"sweeps"* a pair of shoes off the table — a superstition she initially made fun of.

Mr Lyons is a stereotypical middle-class man

1) Mr Lyons is a <u>stereotypical</u> middle-class man of the period. He <u>prioritises</u> work, and sees the house as his <u>wife's</u> "domain".

2) He has <u>little empathy</u> for his workers. He talks about them being "surplus to requirement" — he views them as <u>commodities</u>, not as people.

3) Mr Lyons doesn't understand his <u>wife</u> either. He calls her "<u>woman</u>", and suggests she has <u>stereotypical</u> female problems, like "nerves" or "this depression thing". He doesn't seem to take her worries seriously.

Theme — Money and Social Class

Russell uses the Lyonses to suggest that money can't buy you <u>happiness</u>.

You could argue that it's <u>impossible</u> for Mr Lyons to understand Mrs Lyons' fears, because she won't tell him the <u>truth</u>.

Write about how Russell presents the middle classes...

When Edward dies, both the Lyonses are absent, perhaps because Russell doesn't want us to feel sorry for them. Throughout the play, these middle-class characters don't exactly inspire sympathy.

Character Profile — Mickey Johnstone

Edward thinks Mickey is the best thing since sliced bread — he's mischievous, loyal, knows swear words, and shoots at the private parts of statues. Cool. Act One Mickey does alright. Act Two Mickey — not so much...

As a boy, Mickey is mischievous...

1) Mickey is the twin Mrs Johnstone keeps. He's the <u>youngest</u> child in a large, <u>working-class</u> family, and he's often picked on by his older siblings.

2) Aged seven, Mickey is <u>excited</u> by <u>naughty</u> things. He admires how Sammy "wees straight through the letter box" of the house next door. This shows that he finds misbehaving <u>appealing</u>.

3) He <u>encourages</u> Edward to misbehave as well. He tells him to "take no notice of mothers", and teaches him swear words.

> **Writer's Techniques — Symbolism**
>
> Mickey is carrying a "<u>*toy gun*</u>" when he first appears. This <u>foreshadows</u> the end of the play (see p.17).

4) However, Mickey's mischief is mostly for <u>show</u>. He claims to have "been caught loads of times by a policeman", but is "*terrified*" when it happens for real. This shows that he's naughty to <u>impress</u> other children, <u>not</u> because he actually <u>wants</u> to do wrong.

> **Mickey is...**
>
> - **mischievous** — "Ooh, I dare y', Linda"
> - **loving** — "You're great, you are, Mam."
> - **accepting** — "He's my best friend."

As a teenager, Mickey tries to stop Sammy from robbing the bus conductor. This also shows that he doesn't want to get into trouble, and knows right from wrong.

...but he is also sensitive and loving

1) Mickey has a <u>close</u> relationship with Mrs Johnstone. He is the only one of her children who <u>notices</u> her happiness about the move, and he ends up "smilin'" too — his mood is <u>influenced</u> by hers.

2) He is <u>easily upset</u> by other children. He's "*visibly shaken*" by their chant about dying, and sits "*quietly crying*" while Linda defends him. This demonstrates his <u>sensitive</u> side.

> Before Edward comes along, Mickey is <u>overshadowed</u> by Sammy and his bad behaviour. With Edward, Mickey has the chance to <u>lead</u> as the confident and knowledgeable one.

3) Mickey's sensitive nature also makes him very <u>accepting</u> of others. He instantly makes friends with <u>Edward</u>, not caring that he dresses, acts and speaks differently (see p.39).

Mickey is an insecure teenager

Mickey's worries about his appearance and girls are shared by Edward — see p.38.

Mickey has <u>several</u> insecurities as a fourteen-year-old:

- Mrs Johnstone notices Mickey's "thing for taking blackheads out", and he complains about his "ears that stand out" and hair that's "the colour of gravy". This shows that he's <u>self-conscious</u> about his <u>appearance</u>.

- He lacks confidence around <u>girls</u>, and "the words just disappear" when he tries to tell Linda how he feels.

- He also lacks <u>academic</u> confidence. At school, he "*looks about for help*" to answer a question, and when "*there is none*" he makes a joke. These <u>stage directions</u> suggest that he's covering up his insecurity by misbehaving. (Mickey also struggled as a child — he couldn't "do sums and history" like Edward.)

Character Profile — Mickey Johnstone

Mickey lacks opportunities throughout his life

1) Russell presents Mickey as a <u>victim</u> of the <u>class divide</u>. As a working-class character, he has few opportunities to get a good education or a well-paid job.

2) Mickey lacks <u>educational</u> opportunities:

- He doesn't go to a very good school — it's *"all boredom and futility"*.

- The things he's supposed to learn <u>won't help him</u> in adult life. Mickey says that knowing "what some soddin' pygmies in Africa have for their dinner" won't help him get a <u>job</u>. This is what he's <u>expected</u> to do — no one expects him to go to university like Edward.

3) As an adult, Mickey lacks <u>employment</u> opportunities. He has a <u>menial job</u> putting boxes together, and then gets fired and can't find other work because he <u>lacks skills</u>.

4) Russell emphasises how <u>hard</u> Mickey <u>tries</u> to find work — he's been "walking around all day, every day, lookin' for a job". This makes him seem more of a <u>victim</u>.

Theme — Social Class

Mickey is <u>blamed</u> for the stone-throwing incident, which shows how the law is <u>prejudiced</u> against him.

Britain in the Late Twentieth Century

There was <u>widespread</u> working-class <u>unemployment</u> in the 1970s and 1980s because of the decline of major industries (see p.7).

His desperation and depression build towards a climax

1) Mickey's struggles get <u>worse</u> in Act Two. By the final scene, he's at <u>rock bottom</u>:

In Act Two...	In the final scene...
He comes to <u>resent Edward</u> and his lifestyle. Mickey has had to grow up and take on adult responsibilities, whilst Edward is "still a kid".	His resentment reaches a climax when he finds out that Edward is his twin. His outburst *"begins deep down inside him"*, emphasising his <u>agony</u>.
His unemployment makes him feel <u>desperate</u>. When Sammy tells him he has "nothin'", Mickey turns to crime to provide for his family.	Mickey's at his most desperate. The "<u>one thing left</u>" in his life was Linda, but now he's lost her too. Her affair leaves him with <u>nothing</u>.
Mickey has an <u>emotional breakdown</u>. He's *"silently crying"* when he's arrested, and can't "stop the tears" when he's sentenced.	By the end, Mickey's very <u>emotionally unstable</u>. He constantly asks questions, makes accusations, and alternates between shouting and rambling.

2) When Mickey points a gun at Edward, it's a <u>culmination</u> of all these factors, along with the <u>instability</u> caused by coming off his <u>anti-depressants</u>. His <u>self-esteem</u> is also at an all-time low — he was going to shoot Edward, but says he "can't even do that", and ends up killing Edward by <u>accident</u>.

KEY QUOTE

"...how come you got everything... an' I got nothin'?"

Mickey has a pretty rotten time of it in Act Two, and it seems like most of his struggles are down to a lack of choices and opportunities. Russell uses Mickey to make a point about how important social class can be.

Character Profile — Edward Lyons

Edward's a tricky one to place — he's a Johnstone, he's a Lyons, he's loyal, he's disloyal... you get the picture.

Edward has a privileged but stifled upbringing

1) Edward is the twin that Mrs Johnstone <u>gives away</u>.
He grows up in a <u>middle-class</u> home.

2) Mrs Lyons says she can provide Edward with everything he <u>wants</u> and <u>needs</u>, like "all his own toys" and "silver trays to take meals on". This suggests he has a very <u>luxurious</u> upbringing, which makes him <u>generous</u> and happy to share.

3) However, Edward's upbringing is also very strict. Mrs Lyons keeps him "<u>clean, neat and tidy</u>", and doesn't let him out to play. He's raised to be <u>polite</u> and <u>well-behaved</u>.

Theme — Social Class

Edward has opportunities that Mickey doesn't. His <u>private education</u> leads him to university and a good <u>career</u>.

Edward is...

- **confident** — "Will you be my best friend?"
- **polite** — "Hello, Mrs Johnstone. How are you?"
- **impressionable** — "You say smashing things"

He's comfortable in middle-class and working-class settings

1) Edward <u>rebels</u> against Mrs Lyons by going to Mickey's estate. He finds Mickey <u>exciting</u>, and wants to be more like him. In this way, he rejects his middle-class parents for his working-class friends.

2) Edward <u>fits in</u> with Mickey and Linda very quickly, which could suggest that he's more comfortable in a <u>working-class</u> environment.

Theme — Identity

Edward also seems naturally <u>drawn</u> to Mrs Johnstone. This could hint at his <u>natural identity</u> (see p.40).

3) Despite this, Edward <u>returns</u> to Mr and Mrs Lyons, still dresses <u>smartly</u> and has stereotypical <u>middle-class</u> interests, like reading. This shows that he <u>doesn't</u> become fully immersed in working-class life.

Edward behaves differently depending on who he's with

1) Edward becomes more <u>informal</u> around <u>working-class</u> characters, and his <u>speech</u> starts to change. He says "hi-ya" instead of "hello", and "yeh" instead of "yes".

2) Edward's also comfortable in very <u>formal</u> situations. He's well-educated and a good <u>public speaker</u>. In the final scene, he is confidently arguing his case as a local councillor.

3) This ability to change his speech and behaviour for his environment is a <u>skill</u> that allows Edward to <u>succeed</u>. He can <u>fit in</u> with working-class people, but he can also succeed in a <u>formal career</u>.

Character — Mickey

Mickey <u>doesn't</u> have this skill with formal language, so he is <u>uncomfortable</u> in formal environments. When he bursts in on Edward at the council building, his shouts of "stay where you are!" and "get her out of here, mister, now!" <u>contrast</u> with the calm and formal speech Edward has been making.

Character Profile — Edward Lyons

Edward's loyalty is questionable

It's possible to interpret Edward as both loyal and disloyal, depending on how you view his actions:

Edward loves Linda, but he won't ask her out because of his loyalty to Mickey. He selflessly encourages them to get together.	After he falls out with Mickey, he asks Linda to marry him. He later has an affair with Linda, which is the ultimate betrayal of Mickey.
He's loyal to Mrs Johnstone by treasuring his locket, even when he gets suspended for refusing to let a teacher see it.	However, he fails to keep it a secret as Mrs Johnstone asked, because the other schoolboys know about it. He also gives it to Mrs Lyons without a fight.
He uses his position to get Linda and Mickey a house and Mickey a job.	He does this behind Mickey's back, which makes it seem patronising.

He becomes naive about working-class problems

1) When Edward returns from university, he is full of excitement. His repetition when he talks about "so many parties" and "so many tremendous people" shows how much he's enjoying it.

Writer's Techniques — Structure

Edward tries to offer Mickey money, but Mickey throws it back in his face. This reminds the audience of when Mrs Lyons tried to pay off Mrs Johnstone. Like his mother, Edward comes to think that money fixes problems, and doesn't consider the other person's self-esteem.

2) However, his lifestyle has made him naive. When he suggests that Mickey should just "draw the dole" and "live like a bohemian", he demonstrates a complete lack of understanding of Mickey's situation.

3) Edward has spent too long in a middle-class world, which makes him lose touch with working-class issues. He comes back unable to empathise with his best friend.

He has opportunities, but his personal life is difficult

1) Edward has a good education and access to books, but he struggles to put his knowledge into practice. For example, as a teenager he tells Mickey he's "read about" how to approach girls, but he doesn't actually have a girlfriend.

2) As an adult, Edward still doesn't seem to have a partner — until his affair with Linda, who is his best friend's wife.

3) He doesn't appear to have a close relationship with his parents. Mrs Lyons betrays him by revealing the affair to Mickey, and Edward isn't shown interacting with Mr Lyons at all as a teenager or an adult.

© Donald Cooper/Photostage.co.uk

 Write about Edward's positive and negative qualities...

It would be easy to write that Edward's the good twin, and Mickey's the one who goes off the rails. But remember Edward also betrays Mickey, and sometimes shows a lack of understanding.

Character Profile — Linda

Linda may not be on stage that much, but she plays a very important part in the events of the play.

Linda both conforms to and rebels against gender stereotypes

1) In some ways, Linda is a <u>stereotypical</u> late-twentieth-century girl:

- She has to <u>wait</u> for Mickey to ask her out — she <u>can't initiate</u> the relationship herself.

- She becomes a <u>housewife</u>. Her priorities are her husband and child.

- She is <u>unable</u> to stop Mickey from getting involved with the robbery, suggesting that he makes decisions without her. This shows her lack of <u>control</u>.

Linda is...
- **loyal** — "Oh, leave him alone, you. Y' big worm!"
- **proactive** — "I think I've got Mickey a job"
- **trapped** — "There's a girl inside the woman"

© Nils Jorgensen/REX

2) However, in other ways Linda <u>goes against</u> gender stereotypes:

- She's <u>open</u> about her feelings for Mickey, repeatedly telling him "I love you". In this way she <u>drives</u> their relationship forward.

- She <u>defends</u> Mickey against the other children and, later, the teacher. This is a <u>reversal</u> of gender stereotypes, where the man is expected to look after and defend the woman.

- Linda has to be <u>proactive</u> — she tells Mrs Johnstone "We've got our own place an' I think I've got Mickey a job." Like Mrs Johnstone, Linda has to take on the role of <u>breadwinner</u> as well as housewife.

Linda is torn between Mickey and Edward

1) Linda <u>loves</u> Mickey, but she <u>also loves</u> Edward "in a way". However, she gets pregnant and the decision about who to spend her life with is <u>made for her</u>.

Britain in the Late Twentieth Century

At this time, unmarried pregnant women were expected to <u>marry</u> the father of their child as soon as possible.

2) Once married, she has to deal with Mickey's <u>jail sentence</u>, <u>depression</u> and <u>drug addiction</u>, as well as the <u>boredom</u> of having to wash "a million dishes". The strain of this <u>pushes</u> her towards an affair with Edward.

Theme — Social Class

Linda becomes <u>pregnant</u> almost as soon as she and Mickey start dating. This may be a result of <u>poor education</u> about contraception. Because of her situation, Linda can't truly <u>escape</u> her working-class background.

3) The "girl inside the woman" is desperate to escape the <u>stresses</u> of her adult life. She and Edward act like children together, for example Edward *"mimes firing a gun"* and they are *"kicking up the leaves"*. Edward represents <u>freedom</u> — being with him allows Linda to <u>escape</u> from her problems.

Write about Linda's internal struggle...

For most of the play, Linda is fiercely loyal to Mickey. Her affair with Edward is one of the turning points in the play, pushing Mickey over the edge. In the exam, write about why her dedication to Mickey wavers.

Character Profile — Sammy Johnstone

Sammy's a chap of many talents — long-distance spitting, drawing nude women, shooting people. What a guy.

Sammy has a lot of influence over Mickey

1) In the <u>absence</u> of a father, Mickey sees Sammy as a male <u>role model</u> — he says "I wish I was our Sammy".

2) The children, "*led by Sammy*", scare Mickey, telling him that he's "gonna die". Mickey takes the threat seriously, showing that Sammy can <u>manipulate</u> Mickey's emotions.

3) Sammy <u>persuades</u> Mickey to join in with the robbery, using rhetorical questions like "What have y' got?" and <u>tempting</u> him with money.

4) Even though Mickey <u>looks up</u> to him, Sammy doesn't show much <u>brotherly love</u>. He <u>runs out</u> on Mickey when the petrol station robbery goes wrong, and <u>ignores</u> the "*tears streaming down his face*".

> **Sammy is...**
> - **influential** — "I wish I was our Sammy"
> - **deviant** — "Sammy burnt the school down"
> - **selfish** — "*Sammy splits out the back. Mickey remains silently crying.*"

Sammy's behaviour becomes increasingly deviant

1) Sammy is <u>naughty</u> as a child, and his behaviour becomes <u>steadily worse</u> as he grows up.

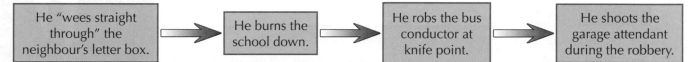

He "wees straight through" the neighbour's letter box.	→	He burns the school down.	→	He robs the bus conductor at knife point.	→	He shoots the garage attendant during the robbery.

2) Although Sammy <u>mocks</u> Mickey and Linda for being "just kids", he doesn't <u>mature</u> as an adult:

- He refers to guns as "<u>shooters</u>".
- He says "Y' don't get up again if one of these hits y'", referencing the <u>game</u> they play as children.
- He makes <u>no effort</u> to find work — he stays on the <u>dole</u>.
- He doesn't take <u>responsibility</u> for his actions — he runs away when the robbery doesn't go to plan.

3) Sammy is a <u>stereotypical</u> working-class youth of the time — he is <u>fulfilling</u> society's expectations of him by turning to a life of crime.

> **Theme — Social Class**
> Sammy can be seen to <u>represent</u> all of Mrs Johnstone's children — the audience don't even learn the names of most of the others. This suggests that, like Sammy, all of her children will have <u>few opportunities</u> in life.

© Nils Jorgensen/REX

"I'm gonna get a real gun soon"

Even as a child, Sammy's desperate to get his hands on a real gun. If only someone had spotted the villainy bubbling away beneath the surface and got him some help. How differently things might have turned out...

Character Profile — The Narrator

The Narrator is a riddle, wrapped in a mystery, inside an enigma. Still, the whole baffling bundle comes packaged in a rather snazzy black suit, so at least standards of elegance and taste are maintained. Phew.

The Narrator is an unpleasant presence

1) He plays a range of <u>unsympathetic</u> roles:

- As the Milkman, he tells Mrs Johnstone "no money, no milk", even though she's <u>pregnant</u>.

- As the Gynaecologist, he <u>abruptly</u> tells Mrs Johnstone that she's "expecting twins". He refers to the twins as "mouths to feed", which plays up to Mrs Johnstone's <u>financial worries</u> and shows that he <u>doesn't sympathise</u> with her situation.

- As the Teacher, he <u>threatens</u> to have Edward "flogged" and <u>humiliates</u> Mickey.

2) He <u>judges</u> Mrs Johnstone at the very start, labelling her a "mother, so cruel". However, her story makes the audience <u>sympathetic</u> towards her, which suggests the Narrator may be unfairly <u>biased</u> against her.

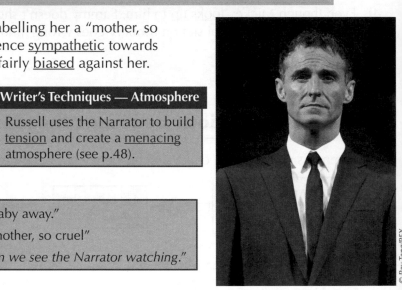

3) He speaks in a <u>threatening</u> way — he repeatedly delivers the <u>ominous</u> line "the devil's got your number". By linking him to the devil and bad-luck omens, Russell makes him seem <u>sinister</u> and <u>malevolent</u>.

Writer's Techniques — Atmosphere

Russell uses the Narrator to build <u>tension</u> and create a <u>menacing</u> atmosphere (see p.48).

The Narrator is...

- **threatening** — "They're gonna take your baby away."
- **judgemental** — "did y' never hear of the mother, so cruel"
- **mysterious** — *"As the light ... begins to dim we see the Narrator watching."*

He's a mysterious character

1) He's usually dressed in <u>black</u> as if he's been to a <u>funeral</u> — this adds to his <u>ominous</u> stage presence, especially given that we know that the play is going to end with the twins' deaths.

Writer's Techniques — Language

The Narrator uses <u>old-fashioned</u> language and <u>rhyme</u>, which sets him apart from the other characters (see p.45 and p.47).

2) He plays several different characters throughout the play, which adds to the air of <u>mystery</u> surrounding him. It also emphasises the fact that the audience don't know <u>who</u> he really is, or <u>how</u> he knows what's going to happen to the twins.

3) He moves in and out of scenes and usually can't be seen or heard by the other characters. This makes him a <u>ghostly</u> figure, which adds to his mysterious and <u>threatening</u> nature.

Write about the characterisation of the Narrator...

It's easy to get caught up in how Russell uses the Narrator for dramatic effect (have a look at p.48 for more). But don't forget to write about him as a <u>character</u> — unsympathetic, judgemental and, well, a bit of a meanie.

Practice Questions

To write a really stunning essay about 'Blood Brothers', you need to know about more than just Mickey and Edward (important as they are). Use these Quick Questions to check you've got to grips with the whole cast.

Quick Questions

1) Which two of these words best describe Mrs Johnstone?
   a) selfish   b) warmhearted   c) wealthy   d) pessimistic   e) powerless

2) Give two pieces of evidence from the play which show that Mrs Johnstone is superstitious.

3) Find two quotes which show that Mrs Lyons is paranoid about Edward's relationship with the Johnstones.

4) Describe Mr Lyons' character in one sentence.

5) How does Mickey feel about Sammy when he's seven years old?

6) What is Edward's job at the end of the play?

7) a) Give one similarity between Mickey and Edward.
   b) Give one difference between Mickey and Edward.

8) Why do Linda and Mickey get married so quickly?

9) Find a quote from Act Two which shows that Sammy doesn't mature as he grows older.

10) Who repeats the line "the devil's got your number"?

11) Write down two minor characters played by the Narrator.

Practice Questions

'Blood Brothers' zips through more than twenty years in the characters' lives, so they go through some pretty big changes. Writing about characters at different points in the play is a great way to show that you've understood the whole thing, and conveniently these In-depth Questions will help you practise just that. Besides, who'd want to be judged on just their seven-year-old self? I valued wearing my favourite jumper over personal hygiene...

In-depth Questions

1) In the prologue, the Narrator describes Mrs Johnstone as a "mother, so cruel".
   Do you think the rest of the play reflects this judgement of her? Explain your answer.

2) a) In what ways are the Johnstones stereotypes of a working-class, late-twentieth-century family?
   b) In what ways are the Lyonses stereotypes of a middle-class, late-twentieth-century family?

3) Compare Mrs Lyons' character when she persuades Mrs Johnstone to give up Edward,
   to her character when she visits Mrs Johnstone in Skelmersdale.

4) Describe how Mickey changes during the course of the play.

5) What signs are there that Linda's life becomes more like Mrs Johnstone's?

6) Mrs Johnstone says that Linda and Edward's affair is "nothing cruel".
   At this point in the play, how far do you sympathise with
   a) Linda?
   b) Edward?
   Explain your answers.

7) 'If Sammy didn't exist, Mickey's life would have been entirely different.'
   How far do you agree with this opinion of Sammy's role in *Blood Brothers*?

8) Explain how Russell presents the Narrator as an unpleasant character.

Practice Questions

Enjoyable as I'm sure you're finding this book, at the end of the day you're reading it because of an exam, so doing some exam-style questions is generally a wise idea. Remember to back up all your points with quotes from the play, and explain them clearly. (If you are reading this book for enjoyment only, you're probably the kind of person who does exam practice for enjoyment as well, so these are for you too, scarily over-studious person.)

Exam-style Questions

1) Read the play from Linda's line "I hate them!" to her line "Come on, gang, let's go." in Act One. With reference to this passage, and the play as a whole, how does Russell present the relationship between Mickey and Linda in *Blood Brothers*?

2) How does Russell create sympathy for Mickey in *Blood Brothers*?

3) 'Mr Lyons, Mrs Lyons and Edward are all used by Russell to present the middle classes in a negative light.'
   To what extent do you agree with this assessment of these characters?

4) Explain the importance of the Narrator in *Blood Brothers*.

5) How does Russell uses the relationships between different characters in the play to explore ideas about parenting?

Section Four — Themes

Money and Social Class

You're going to be hard pushed to write an essay about *Blood Brothers* without mentioning social class. It affects everything that happens in the play, so make sure you've got your head around it.

The Johnstones and the Lyonses are from different social classes

1) Social class is the most important theme in the play. Russell's message is that social class can determine the course of someone's life.

2) Russell first shows class differences between Mrs Johnstone and Mrs Lyons. Mrs Johnstone is a working-class woman. She struggles to care for her children by herself, and can only "just manage to get by", for example she can't afford to pay the milkman.

3) In contrast, Mrs Lyons can afford a cleaner, lives in a large house, and has a husband who is away on business with the "Company". These things establish her as a wealthy, middle-class woman.

> The Johnstones and the Lyonses are class stereotypes. This makes them instantly recognisable, and it puts the issue of class at the front of the audience's mind.

4) When the twins meet, the differences in class and wealth between the two families are reinforced. For example, Edward has plenty of sweets to offer, which Mickey finds amazing, since he's not used to people having extra to share around.

5) The twins' lives are very different because they are brought up in different social classes. Edward Lyons has a good education and goes on to become a local councillor. Mickey Johnstone has a limited education, can't find a job and gets in trouble with the law.

Class is associated with behaviour

'Blood Brothers' on the Stage

Costume is important for showing class and wealth. In most productions, Edward wears a private school uniform or other smart clothes. Mickey's costume is often the wrong size, dirty and full of holes (see p.50).

1) All of the characters in the play believe that people from different classes behave differently.

2) Both mothers link a middle-class upbringing with politeness and good manners. Mrs Johnstone imagines how the child she gives away "wouldn't get into fights" and wouldn't swear.

3) As soon as they meet, the twins seem to fulfil these expectations. Mickey says he's "pissed off" and teaches Edward "the 'F' word". By contrast, Edward is polite and well-spoken.

4) This expectation also leads to class prejudice. When the boys are caught by the policeman, he treats their parents very differently:

- He threatens and patronises Mrs Johnstone, saying that Mickey "was about to commit a serious crime" and "it'll be the courts" if she's not careful.

- He has a drink with Mr Lyons, and says "it was more of a prank, really". He suggests that Edward shouldn't "mix with the likes of them". This shows how the working-class characters are stigmatised.

Stigmatising someone means labelling them in a negative way.

Character — Sammy

Class prejudice works the other way round as well. Sammy judges Edward on his accent and clothes, calling him "a friggin' poshy".

Money and Social Class

The different classes have different opportunities

1) Russell uses <u>sequential scenes</u> to <u>juxtapose</u> the twins' <u>education</u>. This emphasises how <u>different</u> their school lives are.

2) First, Edward is shown at <u>private</u> boarding school. Despite getting suspended over the locket Mrs Johnstone gives him, Edward <u>values</u> his education. He goes to <u>university</u>, which in turn gets him a <u>well-paid job</u> with <u>financial security</u>.

3) In contrast, Mickey's school is "<u>*all boredom and futility*</u>", which seems to support Mickey's belief that it isn't providing him with <u>anything useful</u> for later life. He ends up in a <u>menial job</u> (which he then loses).

4) The middle-class and working-class characters have different attitudes to education, but Russell also suggests that society has <u>different expectations</u> for students from different classes. There is already "<u>talk of Oxbridge</u>" for Edward, even though he's <u>only fourteen</u>. In contrast, Mickey is expected to "<u>get a job</u>" straight away.

> **Theme — Identity**
>
> Russell also uses these sequential scenes to show the <u>similarities</u> between the brothers. Both of them are <u>suspended</u> for being rude to a teacher. Some of their behaviour is similar, even though they've been raised apart (see p.40).

'Oxbridge' is a blend of 'Oxford' and 'Cambridge', two prestigious universities.

Money is power in the play

© Nils Jorgensen/REX

1) In *Blood Brothers*, <u>having money</u> means having the <u>power to control others</u>. Mrs Lyons has power over Mrs Johnstone because she pays her wages.

2) Having money also means having the <u>power to control your own life</u>. Mrs Lyons <u>uses</u> her wealth to persuade Mrs Johnstone to give her a baby.

3) Mrs Lyons can also use money to <u>solve her problems</u> (even if only temporarily). She can afford to <u>move</u> her family to the countryside to get Edward away from the Johnstones, and twice she tries to <u>bribe</u> Mrs Johnstone to stay out of Edward's life.

4) In contrast, the working-class characters are <u>forced</u> into difficult decisions because of their <u>lack of money</u>. Mrs Johnstone <u>can't afford</u> to keep both twins. The <u>promise of money</u> gives Sammy power over Mickey, convincing him to help with the robbery. Sammy <u>tempts him</u> with thoughts of where he could "take Linda" if he had "<u>cash like that</u>".

5) Money may give characters power, but it <u>doesn't</u> bring them <u>happiness</u>. Both families' lives are ruined in the end.

> **Writer's Techniques — Language**
>
> Mrs Johnstone uses <u>monetary language</u> to describe giving Edward away — she worries about the "<u>price</u>" she'll "<u>have to pay</u>". This shows that her decision is motivated by her <u>financial problems</u>. The Narrator later mentions a "price" and "debts to pay" as well, referring back to this moment and <u>reminding</u> the audience that the price will be the twins' deaths.

EXAM TIP

Write about Russell's message about social class...

Russell shows that social class can be a powerful influence on someone's life. Most essays on *Blood Brothers* should mention social class, because it affects the characters, settings and language of the play too.

Fate and Superstition

So, we watch Mickey and Edward having a jolly childhood, all the while knowing that they're headed for an early and violent death. And, of course, the Narrator's there to constantly remind you of that. How cheery.

Mickey and Edward are doomed from the start

1) Fate is referred to <u>throughout</u> *Blood Brothers*:

- The play starts with a <u>prologue</u> (see p.44), where the audience are shown Mickey and Edward's <u>fate</u> (their deaths).

- Throughout the play, the Narrator <u>repeats</u> the line "<u>the devil's got your number</u>", to <u>remind</u> the audience of the twins' <u>destiny</u>.

Make sure you use technical terms, like 'prologue', to show that you understand the features of a play.

2) Through his use of the Narrator and motifs (see p.49), Russell makes sure that Mickey and Edward's fate is constantly in the <u>audience's mind</u>.

Fate repeatedly brings the brothers together

© Donald Cooper/Photostage.co.uk

1) Mickey and Edward <u>keep meeting</u>, despite both mothers' best efforts.

2) Mrs Johnstone stops Mickey from "playin'" near Edward's house. But almost <u>immediately afterwards</u>, Edward finds Mickey by the Johnstones' house. Edward explains that his mother doesn't let him "play down here" either. It's clear that both mothers are <u>trying</u>, and <u>failing</u>, to keep the boys apart.

3) Mrs Lyons <u>moves</u> her family out of Liverpool to <u>get away</u> from the Johnstones, but they end up in the <u>same place</u> when the Johnstones are "rehoused" in Skelmersdale. Factors <u>outside</u> both women's <u>control</u> keep uniting the twins.

Character — Mrs Lyons

Mrs Lyons feels <u>threatened</u> by her <u>lack of control</u>. She becomes <u>paranoid</u>, and feels that Mrs Johnstone is <u>haunting</u> her: "Wherever I go you'll be just behind me... always and for ever and ever like, like a shadow". This emphasises how the two families are <u>bound together</u> by fate.

Mrs Lyons tries to change fate

1) Mrs Lyons senses that Edward is "<u>drawn to</u>" the Johnstones and will always be linked to them. She feels that "<u>something terrible will happen</u>," but this doesn't stop her from trying to <u>prevent</u> it:

- Twice she tries to <u>pay</u> Mrs Johnstone off to get her <u>away</u> from Edward — first when she dismisses her, then when she discovers that the Johnstones are living in Skelmersdale.

- She <u>forbids</u> Edward from playing with Mickey.

- She "<u>*points out*</u>" Linda and Edward's relationship to Mickey, hoping that it'll drive the brothers <u>apart</u>.

Theme — Money

Mrs Lyons is able to <u>take action</u> because she has money. Mrs Johnstone, by contrast, is forced to <u>accept</u> her fate because she is poor.

2) However, when Mrs Lyons reveals the affair to Mickey, this actually <u>prompts</u> him to confront Edward. Her actions have <u>unintended</u> and <u>tragic</u> consequences. This suggests that fate <u>can't be avoided</u>.

Fate and Superstition

Russell shows that superstitious belief can be very powerful

1) Mrs Lyons knows that Mrs Johnstone is superstitious, so she uses this as a <u>weapon</u> to keep Mrs Johnstone <u>silent</u>. She <u>invents</u> a superstition, telling Mrs Johnstone that twins "secretly parted" will <u>die</u> if they <u>find out</u> they are related.

> **Dramatic Techniques in 'Blood Brothers'**
>
> The audience <u>already know</u> that this superstition will come true. When the <u>audience knows</u> something that the <u>characters don't</u>, it is called <u>dramatic irony</u>.

2) However, superstitious belief starts to <u>control</u> Mrs Lyons as well. She is <u>distraught</u> when Mr Lyons puts shoes on the table, and she is <u>driven mad</u> by her obsession with keeping the twins apart. This shows that superstitious belief can be very <u>powerful</u>.

3) <u>Other</u> characters also start to believe in superstition. For example, Mickey teaches Edward that one magpie means <u>sorrow</u>, so Edward gets <u>upset</u> when he sees one. This shows how quickly superstition can spread.

4) The Narrator mentions many other superstitions associated with <u>bad luck</u>, such as "walkin' on the pavement cracks" and "a looking glass cracked". This all adds to a sense of <u>building panic</u>.

Superstition and fate complicate the idea of responsibility

Russell <u>never blames</u> any <u>one character</u> for Mickey and Edward's deaths. Instead, he prompts his audience to decide for themselves, to get them to <u>think</u> about issues like <u>social class</u> and <u>social responsibility</u>.

In the final scene, the Narrator asks if we should "blame **superstition** for what came to pass?" The threat of superstition is there throughout the play, hinting at its part in the twins' deaths.	On the other hand, Russell is not saying that superstitions are real. He shows that it's people's <u>belief</u> in superstition that is powerful, and potentially dangerous.
Fate can also be seen as the cause of the twins' deaths. We have already seen Mickey and Edward's destiny, so it seems inevitable that they will die.	However, there are many points at which this fate could have been <u>changed</u> if a character had acted slightly differently. For example, if Linda had not started an affair with Edward, Mickey may not have shot him.
The Narrator also asks if "what we, the English, have come to know as class" is responsible. Mickey is disadvantaged by his **social class**, and has few opportunities in life. In this way, society is to blame for what happens.	On the other hand, maybe <u>individual characters</u> could have taken more <u>responsibility</u> for helping others. For example, if Mr Lyons hadn't made Mickey redundant, Mickey wouldn't have turned to crime.

 "You know the devil's got your number..."

Yes, thank you Narrator, I think we get it now. All this stuff about debts and prices and the devil and so on can feel a tad repetitive, but that's the idea. Russell is constantly reminding the audience of the twins' fate.

Childhood and Growing Up

Mickey and Edward are desperate to grow up — even being eight years old feels like a dream. When they do get older, however, life isn't exactly the barrel of laughs they'd expected — at least, not for Mickey.

Childhood is presented as a time of innocence

1) Childhood is mostly presented as a <u>carefree</u> part of life. Russell uses <u>recurring imagery</u> of things like sharing sweets and getting up to mischief to create a sense of a <u>never-ending game</u>.

2) Childhood games <u>don't have consequences</u>. If you die, you can simply "cross your fingers" and "count to ten" and you're no longer dead.

3) Sometimes innocence is a source of <u>comedy</u>. For example, Mickey and Edward try to work out what type of plate Sammy has in his head, and decide it can't be a "side plate" because "<u>it's on the top</u>".

Theme — Friendship

Russell also <u>contrasts relationships</u> in childhood and adulthood. As a child, Edward simply asks Mickey to be his "best friend", and <u>that's that</u>. As adults, their relationship becomes <u>more complicated</u>.

4) The children's innocence also acts as a reminder of the <u>adults'</u> <u>problems</u>. Edward doesn't understand why Mrs Johnstone can't buy a new house "<u>just like that</u>", which emphasises how different her <u>financial situation</u> is from his.

5) Childhood is <u>not</u> completely carefree. The Johnstone children are often <u>hungry</u>, and Edward doesn't want to move away but has <u>no choice</u>. Despite this, childhood problems are far <u>less serious</u> than adult problems.

Growing up is portrayed as divisive and difficult

1) Both Mickey and Edward become <u>self-conscious</u> about their <u>appearance</u> as teenagers. They complain about "permanent acne" and "ears that stand out".

2) Both brothers also <u>find girls difficult</u>. Edward has "read about it", and recites a passage of advice to Mickey, but admits that he will "<u>hardly ever see a girl</u>" at boarding school.

3) Mickey, meanwhile, is pursued by Linda, but when he tries to tell her how he feels, "<u>the words just disappear</u>".

4) When they are children, Linda is a <u>friend</u> to both boys, but as they grow up the twins are <u>pushed apart</u> by their feelings for her. It's finding out about Linda and Edward's <u>affair</u> that tips Mickey <u>over the edge</u>.

Character — Mickey

Mickey's <u>desperation</u> to grow up, emphasised by his insistence on being "nearly eight", makes his adult life seem <u>sadder</u>. He stands with *"tears streaming down his face"* after the robbery, as if all his hopes have completely <u>collapsed</u>.

5) The twins are also divided by their different <u>lifestyles</u> as young adults. Mickey says that he "<u>grew up</u>", but Edward "<u>didn't need to</u>". This shows that growing up is about <u>more</u> than getting older — it is also about taking on <u>adult responsibilities</u>. Mickey is forced to do this <u>straight away</u>, but university <u>extends</u> Edward's youth, so he doesn't need to be an adult. This difference pushes them <u>apart</u>.

EXAM TIP

Write about how the characters change as they get older...

Remember that the play covers more than two decades of the characters' lives — we see them go through some pretty big changes in that time. Show the examiner that you've thought about the whole play.

Friendship

The friendship between Mickey, Edward and Linda is one of the most cheerful parts of the play. It's also a nice break from all that "devil's got your number" stuff the Narrator keeps harping on about. For a time, anyway...

Friendships give characters a sense of belonging

1) Mrs Lyons doesn't allow Edward much freedom, but Mickey gives him the <u>childhood</u> he's been missing out on. By calling Edward "<u>Eddie</u>", Mickey <u>welcomes</u> him into a youthful world for the first time. He also <u>claims</u> Edward for himself by renaming him.

© Donald Cooper/Photostage.co.uk

2) Mickey usually has to share everything with his many siblings, but his friendship with Edward gives him something <u>of his own</u>. He makes Edward swear to "defend" and "stand by him", which gives him a sense of <u>security</u>.

Character — Linda

Linda is <u>fiercely loyal</u> to Mickey. She <u>defends</u> him multiple times as a child, and <u>stands by him</u> as a young woman.

3) Mickey, Edward and Linda form a <u>close friendship</u> that is very important to all of them. The Narrator says they feel "<u>innocent, immortal</u>" when they're together aged fifteen.

Friendship crosses class boundaries for the children...

1) As boys, social class <u>means little</u> to Mickey and Edward. Sammy calls Edward "<u>a friggin' poshy</u>", and Mickey replies "<u>No, he's not. He's my best friend</u>", showing how <u>accepting</u> Mickey is.

2) The twins <u>admire</u> the qualities in one another that make them different. They sing about this when they are separated in Act One. Mickey wishes that he could "<u>wear clean clothes, talk properly</u>" like Edward, while Edward wants to "<u>kick a ball and climb a tree</u>" like Mickey.

3) Although they are <u>apart</u> in this scene, the lyrics they sing in 'My Friend' follow the <u>same pattern</u> and <u>melody</u>, which emphasises their <u>closeness</u>.

...but the twins' friendship changes as they get older

1) As children, <u>Mickey</u> has the <u>power</u> in the friendship. He has knowledge that Edward wants, and behaves in a way that Edward admires. When Edward shouts at Mrs Lyons, "<u>you're a fuckoff!</u>", it is clear that he's already <u>strongly influenced</u> by what Mickey says, even when he doesn't know what it means.

Theme — Social Class

The resentment Mickey feels towards Edward is mostly due to social class. Mickey feels <u>cheated</u> because he hasn't had the same <u>opportunities</u> as Edward. Class boundaries drive the twins apart as adults.

2) As adults, Edward holds the <u>influence</u> in Mickey's life. He gets Mickey a house and a job. Mickey <u>resents</u> this, feeling that he "<u>didn't sort anythin' out</u>" for himself, and this contributes to the final confrontation.

KEY QUOTE

"Mickey says smashing things. We're blood brothers..."

It's love at first sight — how sweet. In the space of ten minutes, Edward has gained a new pal with a stunning collection of swear words, the same birthday and uncannily similar facial features. Wait a sec...

Identity

If you haven't already, it's a good idea to cast your eyes over pages 34 and 35 before you tackle this 'ere page.

Identity is linked to upbringing

1) *Blood Brothers* raises questions about whether <u>nurture</u> (upbringing) or <u>nature</u> (genetic make-up) is more important in deciding what a person is <u>like</u> and the <u>course</u> their life follows.

2) The twins are genetically identical, so differences between them must be down to their <u>upbringing</u>:

> **Nurture (upbringing)**
>
> 1) Mickey is quite <u>wild</u>. For example, he runs and jumps around, "*firing*" at Mrs Johnstone and claiming he's "wiped out three thousand Indians". His wildness could be because Mrs Johnstone gives him a lot of <u>freedom</u>. In contrast, Edward is <u>well-behaved</u> (at least to start with). This could be because Mrs Lyons is a <u>strict</u> parent.
>
> 2) Edward is <u>generous</u>, perhaps because he's always had everything he wants. He gives Mickey sweets and a toy gun. Conversely, Mickey is <u>protective</u> of his possessions, because he's had to share everything.

3) However, there are hints that <u>nature</u> is important too:

> **Nature (genetics)**
>
> 1) Some characters have <u>naturally</u> different identities. For example, Mickey and Sammy are raised in the <u>same way</u>, but are still <u>very different</u>.
>
> 2) Edward starts to <u>become more like</u> Mickey <u>very quickly</u>, for example by answering back to Mrs Lyons. This may suggest that this is his 'natural' state. Mrs Lyons seems to pick up on this, and feels that Edward is "<u>drawn to</u>" the Johnstones.

4) Russell seems to suggest that <u>nurture</u> is more important, because the twins' adult lives are so determined by their <u>social class</u>. Mickey's <u>last words</u> suggest this as well — he believes he "could have been" Edward if he'd had a different upbringing.

Some characters want to change their identity

1) Several characters express a desire to <u>be</u>, or to <u>be like</u>, someone else.

2) Mickey has a <u>monologue</u> in which he repeats the line "<u>I wish I was our Sammy</u>". He wants to be Sammy's age and misbehave like him.

3) Mickey and Edward also want to <u>be one another</u>. The twins sing about "<u>my friend</u>" after Edward moves away, and then "<u>that guy</u>" when they see each other in Act Two. It is <u>ironic</u> that they admire each other's appearance, even though they actually look very similar.

> **The Staging of 'Blood Brothers'**
>
> The mothers are <u>another pair</u> of characters who each <u>want what the other has</u>. The <u>melody</u> used for their song 'My Child' is the same as the one used for 'My Friend' and 'That Guy' later in the play.

4) Having songs about identity at different points in the play shows how <u>important</u> this is to the twins. They also sing parts of verses together, showing their <u>mutual desire</u> for the other's identity.

"*I could have been... I could have been him!*"

Scientists use twins to study how upbringing affects things like intelligence. In the play, Russell uses Mickey and Edward, who are genetically <u>identical</u>, to show that upbringing has a huge impact on someone's life.

Gender

Mickey and Edward may be the title characters in *Blood Brothers*, but the play is also about what it means to be a woman and a mother. Russell uses Mrs Johnstone and Mrs Lyons (and Linda) to explore this.

The husbands are mostly absent but have a lot of influence

1) Mr Lyons <u>isn't</u> on stage very often. He is <u>away</u> for nine months when the play begins, and dashes off to <u>work</u> when reading with Edward. This suggests that he <u>doesn't</u> spend much <u>time</u> with the family.

2) However, he still makes the major <u>decisions</u> for his family. Mr Lyons rules out <u>adopting</u> a child, even though his wife wants to adopt. It is Mr Lyons who <u>moves</u> the family to the countryside, and only after talking with the policeman — he <u>dismisses</u> his wife's concerns as "<u>nerves</u>".

3) Mrs Johnstone's husband has <u>walked out</u> on his family, leaving them in <u>poverty</u>. He is not named, and his children never mention him, suggesting he's completely <u>vanished</u>. He has a casual attitude towards having children, telling Mrs Johnstone that they only have to "<u>shake hands</u>" for her to get pregnant, but he takes <u>no responsibility</u> for his children.

> **Background and Context**
>
> Mrs Johnstone's situation is <u>unusual</u>. Most families at this time were made up of a husband and wife and their children. The man went out to work and the woman stayed at home (see p.6).

The two mothers judge themselves against gender roles

1) Mrs Lyons is desperate for a child, and sings about the stereotypical <u>motherly roles</u> that she <u>can't fulfil</u>. She has "dreamed" of all the places she would take her son, and about the "games" and "stories" they'd enjoy. Mrs Lyons sees herself as a <u>failure</u> as a <u>woman</u> because she's childless.

© Donald Cooper/Photostage.co.uk

2) Mrs Johnstone has to fulfil the traditionally <u>male</u> role of <u>breadwinner</u>, as well as being a <u>homemaker</u>. She feels she has <u>failed</u> to provide for her children <u>financially</u>, for example she says to Mickey, "you've not had much of a life with me". She sees herself as failing in the role of '<u>father</u>'.

Linda becomes like Mrs Johnstone

In many ways, Linda <u>turns into</u> another Mrs Johnstone, whose freedom has been taken away by family responsibilities:

- Linda becomes a <u>housewife</u>. In Act Two, she's "*preparing Mickey's working things*" and has "washed a million dishes".

- Linda "sorted" out a <u>house</u> and an <u>income</u> for her and Mickey. In this way, like Mrs Johnstone, Linda is both a homemaker and a <u>breadwinner</u>.

> **Character — Donna Marie Johnstone**
>
> Donna Marie Johnstone also turns into her <u>mother</u>. Mrs Johnstone says "<u>she's / A bit like me</u>", because Donna Marie already has three children at the start of Act Two.

KEY QUOTE

"The house is your domain... I've got a board meeting."

Mrs Lyons' to-do list whilst hubby is away: 1) buy new shoes, 2) ponder loneliness of large house, 3) illegally adopt the cleaner's baby and threaten her into lifelong silence. "Jen, I leave you alone for five minutes...!"

Practice Questions

Surprise, surprise, folks — it's another set of practice questions. They're the perfect way to see how themes are shaping up in your mind. Quick Questions only need quick answers, but try a paragraph for the In-depth ones.

Quick Questions

1) Explain Russell's message about social class in one sentence.

2) Find one quote from the play which shows that:
   a) the Johnstone family are working class.
   b) the Lyons family are middle class.

3) Russell begins the play by showing the audience the twins' deaths.
   What is the technical term for this introductory scene?

4) Which character tries to change fate more than any other?

5) Give two examples of superstitions that are mentioned in the play.

6) Which character has to deal with adult responsibilities first, Mickey or Edward?

7) Find a quote from the play which shows that Edward is influenced by Mickey.

8) Is the following statement true or false?
   Mrs Johnstone is both the breadwinner and the homemaker in her family.

In-depth Questions

1) Explain how money gives characters power in the play.

2) How does Russell show that superstitious belief can be both powerful and influential?

3) In what ways are childhood and adulthood contrasted in the play?

4) Do you think nature or nurture is more important in forming the twins' identities? Why?

5) To what extent does Linda conform to traditional female gender roles?

Practice Questions

Examiners love themes almost as much as they love cake.* This means themes are highly likely to come up in the exam. For each theme in this section, try to jot down a few bullet points of key ideas. Then have a stab at these beauties below. Remember to back up all of your points with quotes from the play, and comment on their effects. You could even do a few of these questions in exam conditions — go wild.

Exam-style Questions

1) "You don't understand anythin', do ye? I don't wear a hat that I could tilt at the world."
   How does Russell use Mickey and Edward to explore ideas about class?

2) 'Mickey and Edward are doomed from the start and nothing can prevent their deaths.'
   How far do you agree with this view?

3) To what extent does Russell present childhood as a time of innocence?

4) 'Mickey and Edward's friendship does them more harm than good.'
   How far do you agree with this statement?

5) At the end of the play, Mickey says to Mrs Johnstone, "Why didn't you give me away?...
   I could have been... I could have been him!"
   To what extent do you think Mickey is right?

6) How does Russell use the characters in the play to explore ideas about gender?

*CGP disclaimer: There is currently no scientific proof that examiners consume more baked goods than workers in any other profession.

Section Five — Writer's Techniques

Structure and Form in 'Blood Brothers'

Structure and form are essential bits of good English essays, so make sure you have something to say about them.

The play has a cyclical structure

1) The play begins at the end, with a <u>prologue</u> showing the twins' <u>deaths</u>.

2) The deaths occur <u>again</u> at the end of the play.

3) The <u>same lines</u> are used at both the start and the end of the play as well. The Narrator asks the audience if they've heard "the story of the Johnstone twins", and Mrs Johnstone <u>repeats</u> "Tell me it's not true". This repetition emphasises Mrs Johnstone's grief and reminds the audience that the tragedy was <u>inevitable</u>.

A prologue is a scene that comes before a story, which usually gives you information about what is to come.

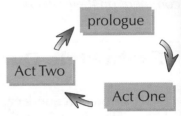

The Narrator appears throughout the play to remind the audience that the twins are going to die. This means that the twins' <u>fate</u> is never far from the audience's mind.

The action flows continuously with no scene breaks

1) Unlike <u>most</u> plays, there are no scene breaks in *Blood Brothers*. The action moves <u>straight</u> from one part of the story to another.

2) This adds to the <u>pace</u> of the play. The audience feel as if the action is <u>speeding</u> towards its inevitable end — the twins' deaths.

3) The lack of scene breaks also means that Russell can show scenes in <u>parallel</u>. For example, the scenes at Edward and Mickey's <u>schools</u> happen side by side. This works well for a play about <u>twins</u> because it emphasises the <u>different paths</u> their lives are taking.

4) Instead of scenes, Russell creates breaks in the action using <u>time jumps</u>. We see the time before the twins' birth, then meet them aged seven, fourteen, eighteen and in their twenties. This prompts the audience to <u>compare</u> the boys at various stages.

Writer's Techniques — Staging

Most productions of *Blood Brothers* use a very simple <u>set</u>, which helps the action to flow smoothly (see p.50).

Some of the action is described in the stage directions

The stage directions describe some of what's <u>happening</u> on stage:

- They specify how characters <u>move</u>. For example, Mrs Johnstone *"dances a few steps"* into Mrs Lyons' house. Russell uses movements like this to show <u>times</u> and <u>locations</u> changing.

- Stage directions describe <u>entrances</u> and <u>exits</u>, such as when *"Mrs Lyons enters... turns Mickey round and points out Edward and Linda"*. This entrance <u>drives</u> the plot forward.

- They can also be used for <u>dramatic effect</u>. For example, the description of Mickey *"breaking through groups of people"*, while Mrs Johnstone runs *"frantically"* after him, <u>builds tension</u> before the final, climactic scene.

- They show <u>transitions</u> in time, such as when Linda, Mickey and Edward are shown ageing from fifteen to eighteen in a <u>montage</u>.

A montage is a series of poses or short scenes which are put together.

Structure and Form in 'Blood Brothers'

Some of the play is written in lyrics

1) Russell first wrote *Blood Brothers* as a straight play, but he then turned it into a <u>musical</u>, so it includes songs.

2) Some songs act like <u>soliloquies</u>, giving the audience an insight into a character's <u>feelings</u>. For example, in Act One Mickey and Edward sing about how much they miss each other.

> *A soliloquy is a speech where one character reveals their thoughts. Other characters can't hear them.*

3) Other songs are used to move the <u>plot</u> along. In Act Two, Mr Lyons <u>fires Mickey</u> in a song.

4) Songs can also highlight the play's <u>themes</u> and <u>motifs</u> (see p.49).

The play is like a cautionary fairy tale

1) In some ways, *Blood Brothers* is a <u>cautionary tale</u>. It's a <u>story</u> used to give a <u>warning</u> — that class divides can ruin lives.

2) In many ways, the Narrator is a traditional <u>storyteller</u>:

- At the <u>start</u> of the play, he asks the audience if they've heard "the <u>story</u> of the Johnstone twins".

- Other characters <u>can't see him</u> most of the time, as if he's telling a story and the other characters are just acting it out.

- His language is quite <u>old-fashioned</u>, and uses lots of <u>rhyming couplets</u> (see p.47). This makes him sound like the narrators in <u>traditional fairy tales</u>, which often have <u>moral</u> messages.

Character — Mrs Lyons

After she goes mad, Mrs Lyons is presented a bit like the <u>wicked witch</u> found in many fairy tales. She lives "on the hill", you should "never ever eat the <u>sweets</u> she gives", and children chant that one look from her will turn your teeth bad and stop your growth, as if she has <u>magical powers</u>.

'Blood Brothers' has some features of a classical tragedy

1) The play has several features in <u>common</u> with classical tragedies:

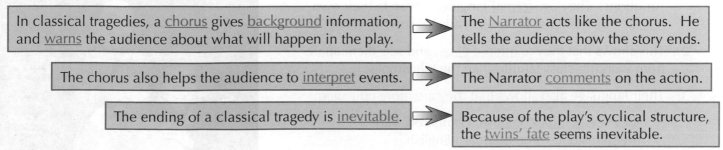

In classical tragedies, a <u>chorus</u> gives <u>background</u> information, and <u>warns</u> the audience about what will happen in the play.	⟹	The <u>Narrator</u> acts like the chorus. He tells the audience how the story ends.
The chorus also helps the audience to <u>interpret</u> events.	⟹	The Narrator <u>comments</u> on the action.
The ending of a classical tragedy is <u>inevitable</u>.	⟹	Because of the play's cyclical structure, the <u>twins' fate</u> seems inevitable.

2) However, the play also <u>differs</u> from a classical tragedy. Classical tragedies focus on <u>one central character</u>, who brings about their <u>own downfall</u> because of a <u>fatal flaw</u>. In *Blood Brothers*, there <u>isn't</u> one central character, and it's up for <u>debate</u> what causes the death of the twins (see p.37).

"*Tell me it's not true, / Say it's just a story...*"
Whilst it explores real issues, Russell reminds us that the play <u>is</u> just a story — it's like a tale to stop kids doing stuff. Instead of 'The Boy Who Cried Wolf', this is 'The Relationship Ruined by Social Class'. Not so catchy.

Section Five — Writer's Techniques

Language in 'Blood Brothers'

Language! Language language language. Whatever you do in the exam (chew pens, juggle monkeys, stare out of the window at the better world that awaits), don't forget to mention language. Right, you may read on.

The Johnstone family use local speech

1) Russell makes the Johnstones' dialogue very realistic to set the scene — they talk in the way that people would have talked on a council estate in Liverpool. Russell uses:

- non-standard spellings — words are spelt in the way that the Johnstones would actually pronounce them, for example "innit" (isn't it) and "gonna" (going to).

- non-standard pronouns — Mickey uses the word "me" instead of "my".
  He also says "Gis a sweet", meaning "give us", because he's using "us" instead of "me".

- dialect words — the Johnstone children call their mother "Mam" or "Ma",
  and refer to one another as "our Sammy" and "our Donna Marie".

- omission — all of the Johnstones leave letters off the end of words. For example,
  Mickey says "D' they call y' Eddie?" instead of "Do they call you Eddie?"

- expletives — the Johnstones swear a lot, especially Sammy.

2) The Johnstones' language shows their social class. They represent a working-class community, so through them the audience can hear the council estate coming to life.

> **Writer's Techniques — Staging**
>
> Actors playing the Johnstones also speak in a Liverpudlian ('scouse') accent.

3) The Johnstones also use more poetic language than the Lyonses.
For example, Mrs Johnstone uses hyperbole, saying "it would take you a week just to reach the far side" of her new garden. This reflects her optimistic personality.

Hyperbole is exaggerated language.

The Lyons family use formal language

1) The Lyons family's language doesn't include local variations. They use formal language, even in their own home. For example, Mr Lyons calls his son "old chap".

2) This shows that they're middle class, and sets them apart from working-class families like the Johnstones.

3) Their language also shows that they are more educated:

- they use Standard English, compared with the Johnstones' non-Standard English.

- they often use formal sentence structures, such as when Mrs Lyons asks, "Edward, wherever did you hear such a thing?" in response to his question about the "bogey man".

> **Character — Mrs Lyons**
>
> Mrs Lyons' language changes throughout the play, from authoritative and confident, to frantic and emotional. This shows her descent into madness (see p.23).

> Mr and Mrs Lyons call Edward by his full name, not an informal nickname. He calls them "Mummy" and "Daddy", even as a teenager, which is more common among the middle classes.

Language in 'Blood Brothers'

The Narrator's language sets him apart

1) The Narrator's language is quite <u>formal</u> and <u>old-fashioned</u> — for example, he says "when a mother cried / My own dear sons lie slain". However, he can also be <u>informal</u> — he drops the <u>consonants</u> from the ends of words, and uses words like "<u>gonna</u>".

2) This makes the Narrator <u>classless</u>. The other characters in the play are clearly working class or middle class, but he <u>doesn't fit</u> neatly into either class. This sets him <u>apart</u> from the others, and makes him seem <u>mysterious</u>.

3) He also speaks a lot in <u>rhyming couplets</u>, which makes his language <u>less realistic</u>. This emphasises that he is a <u>storyteller</u> (see p.45), and creates the impression that he has <u>authority</u> and <u>wisdom</u>.

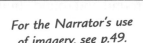

For the Narrator's use of imagery, see p.49.

Rhymes can be playful but also haunting

1) Many of the rhymed line endings in Blood Brothers are quite <u>playful</u>. For example, Mickey sings about how Edward "Always had sweets to share, (he) / Knew every word in the <u>dictionary</u>."

2) At other times, rhymes can be quite <u>haunting</u>. The children chant a superstition at Mickey, saying he'll "<u>die</u>" and "<u>fry</u>" in hell for swearing. The <u>rhyme pattern</u> shifts the <u>mood</u> from a childish game to something nasty.

> Rhymes can also show the <u>relationship</u> between two characters. For example, Mrs Johnstone and Mrs Lyons finish <u>one another's</u> rhymes about "silver trays to take meals on" and "a bike with *both* wheels on". This shows that they're building the <u>same dream</u>.

There is a lot of repetition in the play

Some of the most important lines in the play are <u>repeated</u> or <u>referred to</u> at other points:

"the whole thing's just a game"	⇨	As part of the children's game, this line emphasises the <u>innocence</u> of childhood. The Narrator references it <u>later</u>, after Sammy has actually killed someone, which highlights the <u>loss of innocence</u> in growing up.
"the devil's got your number"	⇨	This line reminds the audience that the twins are <u>doomed</u>, which creates an <u>ominous</u> atmosphere. By mentioning the devil, it makes the <u>superstition</u> seem powerful, suggesting that no one can escape their <u>fate</u>.
"a debt is a debt, and must be paid"	⇨	For Mrs Johnstone, this "debt" represents her <u>lack of money</u> and her <u>regret</u> about giving Edward up. The Narrator's references to "debts to pay" act as a reminder of the "<u>price</u>" of what she did.

Mention how Russell uses language to develop characters...

You don't need to see this play to know what the characters are like, because their dialogue is so distinctive. Write about how Russell uses language to show class (or to make the Narrator seem strange and solitary).

Atmosphere and Mood

What's that? You're enjoying a nice happy scene about young love or the wonders of childhood friendship? Sounds like the perfect moment for a gentle reminder of impending doom. Thanks, Willy. Thanks.

The Narrator is important for creating atmosphere

1) Russell uses the Narrator as a <u>dramatic device</u> to provide:

   • <u>atmosphere</u> — whilst Linda, Mickey and Edward are enjoying teenage life, the Narrator mentions the "price" Linda will pay, and the "fate" that awaits them all. This creates a <u>menacing</u> atmosphere, which <u>contrasts</u> with the characters' freedom and happiness.

   • <u>pace</u> — the Narrator's speech about Mickey as a "mad man running round and round" builds to a <u>climax</u>, increasing the pace and creating an atmosphere of <u>danger</u> and <u>panic</u>.

   • <u>tension</u> — the Narrator's repeated references to the "devil", the "broken looking glass" and other bad luck <u>omens</u> create tension throughout the play.

> **Writer's Techniques — Staging**
>
> The Narrator wears <u>black</u> in most productions. This makes him <u>shady</u> and almost <u>invisible</u>. It also makes him look like he's been to a <u>funeral</u>, which acts as a visual reminder of the prologue.

2) Other characters <u>can't see</u> or <u>hear</u> the Narrator most of the time. This makes him an <u>unsettling</u> presence on stage, which again contributes to a <u>tense</u> atmosphere.

The mood is darker in Act Two than in Act One

1) There are <u>moments</u> of darkness and threat in Act One (such as when the mothers make their pact), but there are also many lighthearted ones. The twins are children, so there are lots of <u>playful</u>, <u>humorous</u> scenes which create a <u>lighter mood</u>.

2) In <u>Act Two</u>, however, the play begins to <u>speed</u> towards its <u>tragic conclusion</u>. Mrs Johnstone seems happy at the start of the Act, but the Narrator quickly appears as the bus conductor to remind her that "No one gets off without the price bein' paid." This creates a <u>threatening</u> atmosphere.

3) From this point on, lighthearted scenes are immediately <u>counteracted</u> by darker ones. For example, Mickey and Linda's wedding is followed by Mickey getting fired, so their happiness seems <u>short-lived</u>.

> **Writer's Techniques — Structure**
>
> Lots of plays follow this <u>structure</u> — a slower, often longer first half, followed by a second half that moves quickly towards the conclusion.

4) The Narrator's repeated line about the devil also changes in Act Two, implying that the devil is moving <u>gradually closer</u> to the characters. This suggests that the tragic ending is <u>fast</u> approaching:

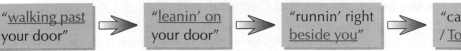

| "<u>walking past</u> your door" | "<u>leanin' on</u> your door" | "runnin' right <u>beside you</u>" | "callin' your number up today / <u>Today</u> / <u>Today</u> / <u>TODAY</u>!" |

"Did you forget about the reckoning day?"

"Mwahaha," says the Narrator, "not so fast." Whenever anyone's starting to enjoy themselves, you can count on the Narrator to ruin the mood. He's your classic fun sponge. Someone needs to book him a holiday.

Imagery and Symbolism

The play is more packed with imagery and symbolism than the Johnstones' suitcases. Here are a few highlights.

Becoming blood brothers is a symbolic moment

Edward and Mickey becoming "blood brothers" is one of the most <u>important moments</u> in the play:

- it <u>symbolises</u> their <u>friendship</u> and the bond between them. Both twins <u>refer</u> to being blood brothers later in the play, which shows how important their bond is to them.

- it <u>demonstrates</u> their openness and acceptance of one another (see p.39).

- it's <u>ironic</u>, because they're <u>actually</u> brothers.

> **Writer's Techniques — Structure**
>
> When the twins swear to "stand by each other" it creates <u>dramatic irony</u>, because the audience knows that they will die together.

Russell uses three main motifs

1) **Dancing** initially represents the <u>happiness</u> of being <u>young</u> and <u>free</u>, particularly for Mrs Johnstone. But later in the play, she says that Mickey's mind has "<u>gone dancing</u>". By using a motif associated with being happy to describe Mickey's depression, Russell makes it seem even <u>worse</u>.

2) **Guns** are used to highlight a <u>loss of innocence</u>. In childhood, guns are seen as <u>fun toys</u>. In adulthood, however, they are <u>highly destructive</u> — three people are shot dead.

> **Character — Sammy**
>
> As an adult, Sammy calls his gun a "<u>shooter</u>", as if he's playing a part in a film. This shows how <u>dangerous</u> he is — he <u>speaks like a child</u>, but he's the owner of <u>lethal</u> weapons.

3) **Marilyn Monroe** represents <u>happiness that doesn't last</u>. Mrs Johnstone was "lovelier than Marilyn Monroe", but her husband left her when she became "twice the size of Marilyn Monroe."

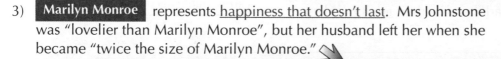

Marilyn Monroe was a glamorous film star who later became addicted to drugs and died from an overdose. When Mickey's addiction is <u>compared</u> to Monroe's, it hints that <u>his death</u> is also approaching.

The Narrator uses lots of imagery

1) The Narrator uses lots of imagery associated with <u>superstition</u>, such as "pavement cracks", a "black cat" and a "full moon". These are all images associated with <u>bad luck</u>, which reminds the audience that something bad is going to happen.

> **Writer's Techniques — Language**
>
> Mrs Johnstone also uses imagery, which makes her language more <u>poetic</u> (see p.46).

2) The Narrator also uses <u>seasonal imagery</u>. When the friends are teenagers, "it seems that summer's never coming to an end", which links their <u>happiness</u> with <u>summer</u>. When Linda becomes pregnant, he says that "<u>winter</u> broke the promise that summer had just made," suggesting that their freedom and joy are <u>over</u>.

EXAM TIP

Mention the repeating symbols and images...

If you spot something that's repeated in *Blood Brothers* — a symbol, an image or a line — it's there for a reason. Russell is probably asking you to compare characters, ideas or themes. No rest for the wicked, eh.

'Blood Brothers' on the Stage

Blood Brothers is a hugely successful musical, and has been performed all over the world. All these different productions have a few key things in common, though, and you can write about those in your exam.

The staging is simple but creates tension

1) The staging for *Blood Brothers* is usually very <u>simple</u>. Most productions only use a <u>small</u> amount of <u>set</u>, which <u>doesn't change</u> much throughout the play.

2) This creates a more <u>intense atmosphere</u> — the events of over twenty years are played out in the <u>same space</u>.

Writer's Techniques — Structure

A limited set helps the action to flow <u>smoothly</u>, with no scene breaks.

3) <u>Background music</u> and <u>sound effects</u> are also used to add <u>tension</u>:

- When Mrs Johnstone swears on the Bible, there is *"a bass note, repeated as a heartbeat"*. This emphasises the <u>significance</u> of this moment, and highlights Mrs Johnstone's <u>fear</u>.

- The music *"pulsates and builds"* as Mickey runs round the town, and then *"stops abruptly"* on the word "TODAY!" This marks the <u>shift</u> from Mickey's frenzy to Edward's formal speech in the council chamber, and highlights the <u>difference</u> in the brothers' situations. It also creates a <u>dramatic pause</u> before the final confrontation.

The same actors play the characters throughout

1) The <u>same actors</u> play Mickey, Edward, Linda and Sammy throughout the play. This makes it easier for the audience to <u>recognise</u> the characters and <u>identify</u> with them.

Theme — Childhood and Growing Up

Using the same actors also works in the <u>opposite way</u> — in tense adult scenes, the audience see the same people they saw enjoying childhood. This highlights their <u>loss of innocence</u>.

2) It also acts as another <u>reminder</u> of the prologue for the audience — even in the childhood scenes, we can already <u>visualise</u> the characters as adults, with their <u>adult problems</u>.

Costumes are representative of social class

1) <u>Mickey</u> and <u>Edward</u> are usually dressed as <u>opposites</u>. Mickey's clothes are scruffy and don't fit him. Edward usually appears in a smart school uniform, or a shirt and smart trousers.

2) Mrs Johnstone and Mrs Lyons also have <u>contrasting</u> costumes. Mrs Johnstone is often shown in <u>practical</u> clothing, such as an apron, to emphasise that she's a <u>working</u> woman. Mrs Lyons, on the other hand, usually wears <u>expensive-looking</u> outfits, which show her <u>wealth</u>.

© Donald Cooper/Photostage.co.uk

Theme — Social Class

The two families are <u>stereotypes</u> of their social classes (see p.34). This means they are also stereotypically dressed.

KEY QUOTE *"He was clean, neat and tidy, / From Monday to Friday..."*

You'll notice that different *Blood Brothers* productions use quite similar costumes. It's not that the costume departments are tediously unoriginal — it's because costume is so important for showing social class.

Practice Questions

Time for a few questions to test your knowledge. I promise none of them are about the diet of the Boro Indian of the Amazon Basin (which includes the leaves of coca plants, in case you were wondering.)

Quick Questions

1) "*Blood Brothers* has a cyclical structure." What does this mean?

2) At which of these ages do we not see the twins?
   a) seven
   b) ten
   c) fourteen

3) Give one feature that *Blood Brothers* has in common with classical tragedies.

4) Find one example from the play of a line that is repeated.

5) In which act is the mood darker, Act One or Act Two?

6) a) Give one example of a motif in *Blood Brothers*.
   b) Explain in one sentence what this motif represents.

7) Is the following statement true or false?
   The set for 'Blood Brothers' needs to be very complex in order to build tension.

In-depth Questions

1) In what ways is *Blood Brothers* like a cautionary fairy tale?

2) Explain how the language of the Johnstone family differs from that of the Lyons family, and what this tells you about the two families.

3) How does Russell use the Narrator to create atmosphere in the play?

4) Explain how motifs are used to show Mickey's transition from innocent boy to troubled adult.

5) Choose two characters from the play, and explain what costumes you would choose for them.

Practice Questions

Like Edward, it's time to study up and get ahead — who knows, one day you could even rise to the dizzying heights of local councillor... What would be even better, though, would be to turn over your English exam paper and realise that the 'Blood Brothers' question is just like one you've done before. I'll let you pause to savour that idea. Once it's sunk in, have a go at the stimulating specimens below. Don't forget to plan first.

Exam-style Questions

1) Explain how the structure and form of *Blood Brothers* contribute to the play's tense atmosphere.

2) How does Russell use language to develop the characters in the play?

3) 'The moment at which Edward and Mickey become "blood brothers" is the most important symbolic event in the play.' How far do you agree with this view?

4) Why are rhyme, repetition and motifs important language features in *Blood Brothers*?

5) Choose a passage from the play that you find especially tense.
How does Willy Russell build tension and drama in this passage?

Exam Preparation

Getting to know the text will put you at a massive advantage in the exam. It's not enough just to read it though — you've got to get to grips with the nitty-gritty bits. It's all about gathering evidence...

The exam questions will test four main skills

You will need to show the examiner that you can:

1) Write about the text in a <u>thoughtful way</u> — <u>picking out</u> appropriate <u>examples</u> and <u>quotations</u> to back up your opinions.

> Not all exam boards will test you on this. Check with your teacher.

2) <u>Identify</u> and <u>explain</u> features of the play's <u>form</u>, <u>structure</u> and <u>language</u>. Show how Russell uses these to create meanings and effects.

3) <u>Link</u> the story to its <u>cultural, social and historical background</u> (i.e. late-twentieth-century Britain).

4) Write in a <u>clear</u>, <u>well-structured</u> way. <u>5%</u> of the marks in your English Literature exams are for <u>spelling</u>, <u>punctuation</u> and <u>grammar</u>. Make sure that your writing is as <u>accurate</u> as possible.

Preparation is important

1) It's <u>important</u> to cover <u>all</u> the <u>different sections</u> of this book in your <u>revision</u>. You need to make sure you <u>understand</u> the text's <u>context</u>, <u>plot</u>, <u>characters</u>, <u>themes</u> and <u>writer's techniques</u>.

2) In the <u>exam</u>, you'll need to <u>bring together</u> your <u>ideas</u> about these topics to answer the question <u>quickly</u>.

3) Think about the different <u>characters</u> and <u>themes</u> in the text, and write down some <u>key points</u> and <u>ideas</u> about each one. Then, find some <u>evidence</u> to support each point — this could be something from <u>any</u> of the <u>sections</u> in this book. You could set out your evidence in a <u>table</u> like this:

Character: Mickey Johnstone	
Playful/mischievous child	Often seen playing games with other children. Wants to mimic Sammy's bad behaviour (e.g. weeing through letterbox).
Relationship with Edward	Instantly accepting of Edward — suggests becoming "blood brothers". Close relationship through most of play, but comes to resent him later.
Contrast Act One and Act Two	Love of life vs. depression. Loses job, sent to jail, anti-depressants. He's "feelin' fifteen years older" — highlights contrast with youthfulness.
Motifs linked with Mickey	Guns — first seen holding toy gun. Foreshadows shooting Edward/ own death. Marilyn Monroe — happiness changing to addiction.
Presented as victim of society	Lacks opportunities throughout, and stigmatised by society. Makes effort but fails, e.g. "walking around all day, every day, lookin' for a job".

Preparing to succeed — a cunning plot indeed...

Knowing the plot inside out will be unbelievably helpful in the exam. It'll help you to stay calm and make sure you write a brilliant answer that positively glitters with little gems of evidence. The exam's just a chance for you to show off...

The Exam Question

This page deals with how to approach an exam question. The stuff below will help you get started on a <u>scorching exam answer</u>, more scorching than, say, a phoenix cooking fiery fajitas in a flaming furnace.

Read the question carefully and underline key words

1) The style of question you'll get depends on which <u>exam board</u> you're taking.

2) Read all the <u>instructions</u> carefully. Make sure you know <u>how many</u> questions you need to answer and <u>how much time</u> you should spend answering each one.

3) If the question has <u>more than one part</u>, look at the total number of marks for each bit. This should help you to plan your <u>time</u> in the exam.

4) <u>Read</u> the question at least <u>twice</u> so you completely understand it. <u>Underline</u> the key words. If you're given an <u>extract</u>, underline <u>important</u> words or phrases in that too.

Henry didn't read the weather report carefully enough when planning his weekend activities.

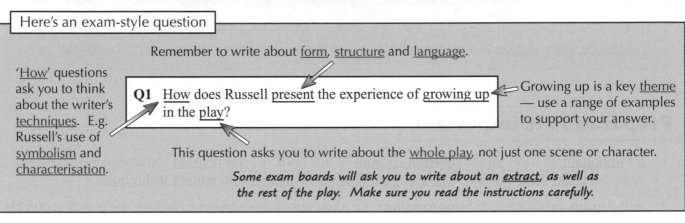

Here's an exam-style question

Remember to write about <u>form</u>, <u>structure</u> and <u>language</u>.

'<u>How</u>' questions ask you to think about the writer's <u>techniques</u>. E.g. Russell's use of <u>symbolism</u> and <u>characterisation</u>.

Q1 <u>How</u> does Russell <u>present</u> the experience of <u>growing up</u> in the <u>play</u>?

Growing up is a key <u>theme</u> — use a range of examples to support your answer.

This question asks you to write about the <u>whole play</u>, not just one scene or character.

Some exam boards will ask you to write about an <u>extract</u>, as well as the rest of the play. Make sure you read the instructions carefully.

Get to know exam language

Some <u>words</u> come up time and again in <u>exam questions</u>. Have a look at some <u>specimen</u> questions, pick out words that are <u>often used</u> in questions and make sure that you <u>understand</u> what they mean. You could <u>write a few down</u> whilst you're revising. For example:

Question Word	You need to...
Explore / Explain	Show <u>how</u> the writer deals with a <u>theme</u>, <u>character</u> or <u>idea</u>. Make several <u>different</u> points to answer the question.
How does	Think about the <u>techniques</u> or <u>literary features</u> that the author uses to get their point across.
Give examples	Use <u>direct quotes</u> and describe <u>events</u> from the text in your own words.
Refer to	Use an <u>extract</u> from the play as <u>part</u> of your answer. Only some exam boards will ask you to do this — check with your teacher.

The advice squad — the best cops in the NYPD...

Whatever question you're asked in the exam, your answer should touch on the main characters, themes, structure and language of the text. All the stuff we've covered in the rest of the book in fact. It's so neat, it's almost like we planned it.

Planning Your Answer

I'll say this once — and then I'll probably repeat it several times — it is absolutely, completely, totally and utterly essential that you make a plan before you start writing. Only a fool jumps right in without a plan...

Plan your answer before you start

1) If you plan, you're less likely to forget something <u>important</u>.

2) A good plan will help you <u>organise</u> your ideas — and write a good, <u>well-structured</u> essay.

3) Write your plan at the <u>top of your answer booklet</u> and draw a <u>neat line</u> through it when you've finished.

4) <u>Don't</u> spend <u>too long</u> on your plan. It's only <u>rough work</u>, so you don't need to write in full sentences. Here are a few <u>examples</u> of different ways you can plan your answer:

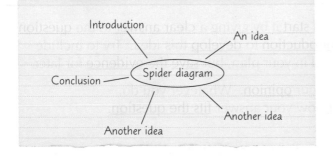

<u>Bullet points...</u>
- Introduction...
- An idea...
- The next idea...
- Another idea...
- Yet another idea...
- Conclusion...

Include bits of evidence in your plan

1) <u>Writing</u> your essay will be much <u>easier</u> if you include <u>important quotes</u> and <u>examples</u> in your plan.

2) You could include them in a <u>table</u> like this one:

3) <u>Don't</u> spend <u>too long</u> writing out quotes though. It's just to make sure you <u>don't forget</u> anything when you write your answer.

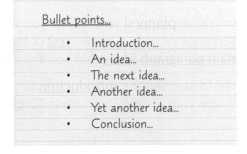

A point...	Quote to back this up...
Another point...	Quote...
A different point...	Example...
A brand new point...	Quote...

Structure your answer

Introduction → Middle Section — paragraphs expanding your argument. → Conclusion

1) Your <u>introduction</u> should give a brief answer to the question you're writing about. Make it clear how you're going to <u>tackle the topic</u>.

2) The <u>middle section</u> of your essay should explain your answer in detail and give evidence to back it up. Write a <u>paragraph</u> for each point you make. Make sure you <u>comment</u> on your evidence and <u>explain how</u> it helps to <u>prove</u> your point.

3) Remember to write a <u>conclusion</u> — a paragraph at the end which <u>sums up</u> your <u>main points</u>. There's <u>more</u> about introductions and conclusions on the <u>next page</u>.

Dirk finally felt ready to tackle the topic.

To plan or not to plan, that is the question...

The answer is yes, yes, a thousand times yes. Often students dive right in, worried that planning will take up valuable time. But 5 minutes spent organising a well-structured answer is loads better than pages of waffle. Mmm waffles.

Writing Introductions and Conclusions

Now you've made that plan that I was banging on about on the last page, you'll know what your main points are. This is going to make writing your introduction as easy as pie. Chocolate fudge pie to be precise.

Get to the point straight away in your introduction

1) First, you need to <u>work out</u> what the question is <u>asking you</u> to do:

> ### How is the character of Mrs Lyons important in the play?
>
> The question is <u>asking you</u> to think about the <u>role</u> of <u>Mrs Lyons</u> in the play. Plan your essay by thinking about <u>how</u> Mrs Lyons <u>drives</u> the plot forward, and <u>links</u> to the play's <u>key themes</u>.

2) When you've <u>planned</u> your essay, you should <u>start</u> it by giving a <u>clear answer</u> to the <u>question</u> in a sentence or two. Use the <u>rest</u> of the <u>introduction</u> to <u>develop</u> this idea. Try to include the <u>main paragraph ideas</u> that you have listed in your plan, but <u>save</u> the <u>evidence</u> for later.

3) You could also use the <u>introduction</u> to give your <u>opinion</u>. Whatever you do, make sure your introduction makes it <u>clear</u> how your answer <u>fits the question</u>.

Your conclusion must answer the question

1) The <u>most important</u> thing you have to do at the <u>end</u> of your writing is to <u>summarise</u> your <u>answer</u> to the question.

2) It's your <u>last chance</u> to persuade the examiner, so make your <u>main point</u> again.

3) Use your <u>last sentence</u> to really <u>impress</u> the <u>examiner</u> — it will make your essay <u>stand out</u>. You could <u>develop</u> your own <u>opinion</u> of the text or <u>highlight</u> which of your <u>points</u> you thought was the most <u>interesting</u>.

The examiner was struggling to see the answer clearly.

Use the question words in your introduction and conclusion

1) Try to use <u>words</u> or <u>phrases</u> from the <u>question</u> in your introduction and conclusion.

> ### How does Russell use language to show class divides in the play?

2) This will show the examiner that you're <u>answering the question</u>.

> Russell uses language in 'Blood Brothers' to establish differences between characters from different social classes.

The first sentence of the introduction gives a clear answer, which will lead on to the rest of the essay.

3) This will also help you keep the question <u>fresh in your mind</u> so your answer doesn't <u>wander off-topic</u>.

I've come to the conclusion that I really like pie...

To conclude, the introduction eases the examiner in gently, whilst the conclusion is your last chance to impress. But remember — the examiner doesn't want to see any new points lurking in those closing sentences.

Writing Main Paragraphs

So we've covered the beginning and the end, now it's time for the meaty bit. The roast beef in between the prawn cocktail and the treacle tart. This page is about how to structure your paragraphs. It's quite simple...

P.E.E.D. is how to put your argument together

Remember to start a new paragraph every time you make a new point.

1) P.E.E.D. stands for: Point, Example, Explain, Develop.

2) Begin each paragraph by making a point. Then give an example from the text (either a quote or a description). Next, explain how your example backs up your point.

3) Finally, try to develop your point by writing about its effect on the audience, how it links to another part of the text or what the writer's intention is in including it.

Use short quotes to support your ideas

1) Don't just use words from the play to show what happens in the plot...

> Mrs Lyons is manipulative. She asks "with two more children how can you possibly avoid some of them being put into care?"

This just gives an example from the text without offering any explanation or analysis.

2) Instead, it's much better to use short quotes as evidence to support a point you're making.

3) It makes the essay more fluent and focused if most quotes are embedded in your sentences.

It's better to use short, embedded quotes as evidence. Then you can go on to explain them.

> Mrs Lyons manipulates Mrs Johnstone into giving her a child. She uses imperatives like "give one of them to me!" and "tell me". These commanding phrases establish her authority over Mrs Johnstone, making it harder for Mrs Johnstone to refuse.

Get to know some literary language

1) Using literary terms in your answer will make your essay stand out — as long as you use them correctly.

2) When you're revising, think about literary terms that are relevant to the text and how you might include them in an essay. Take a look at the table below for some examples.

Literary Term	Definition	Example
Foreshadowing	When the author hints at a future event.	When we first see Mickey he is *"carrying a toy gun"*.
Prologue	A scene that comes before a story, which usually gives information about what is to come.	The prologue in *Blood Brothers* shows the twins' deaths, to establish the importance of fate in the play.
Hyperbole	Exaggerated language	"The air is so pure, / You get drunk just by breathing"

This page is so exciting — I nearly...

Now now, let's all be grown-ups and avoid the obvious joke. It's a good way of remembering how to structure your paragraphs though. Point, Example, Explain, Develop. Simple. Maybe we could make a rap or something... anyone?

In the Exam

Keeping cool in the exam can be tricky. But if you take in all the stuff on this page, you'll soon have it down to a fine art. Then you can stroll out of that exam hall with the swagger of an essay-writing master.

Don't panic if you make a mistake

1) Okay, so say you've timed the exam beautifully. Instead of putting your feet up on the desk for the last 5 minutes, it's a good idea to <u>read through</u> your <u>answers</u> and <u>correct any mistakes</u>...

2) If you want to get rid of a mistake, <u>cross it out</u>. <u>Don't scribble</u> it out as this can look messy. Make any corrections <u>neatly</u> and <u>clearly</u> instead of writing on top of the words you've already written.

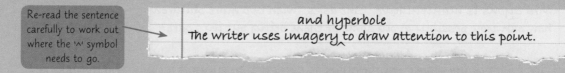

The author uses various literary ~~teknikues~~ techniques to explore this theme.

This is the clearest way to correct a mistake. Don't be tempted to try writing on top of the original word.

3) If you've <u>left out</u> a <u>word</u> or a <u>phrase</u> and you've got space to add it in <u>above</u> the line it's missing from, write the missing bit above the line with a '^' to show exactly where it should go.

Re-read the sentence carefully to work out where the '^' symbol needs to go.

The writer uses imagery to draw attention to this point.
(and hyperbole)

4) If you've left out whole <u>sentences</u> or <u>paragraphs</u>, write them in a <u>separate section</u> at the <u>end</u> of the essay. Put a <u>star</u> (*) next to both the <u>extra writing</u> and the <u>place</u> you want it to go.

Always keep an eye on the time

1) It's surprisingly <u>easy</u> to <u>run out of time</u> in exams. You've got to leave <u>enough time</u> to answer <u>all</u> the questions you're asked to do. You've also got to leave enough time to <u>finish</u> each essay properly — with a <u>clear ending</u>.

2) Here are some <u>tips</u> on how to <u>avoid</u> running out of time:

- Work out <u>how much time</u> you have for each part of your answer <u>before</u> you <u>start</u>.
- Take off a few minutes at the beginning to <u>plan</u>, and a <u>few minutes</u> at the end for your <u>conclusion</u>.
- Make sure you have a <u>watch</u> to <u>time yourself</u> — and keep checking it.
- Be <u>strict</u> with yourself — if you spend <u>too long</u> on one part of your answer, you may run out of time.
- If you're <u>running out of time</u>, keep <u>calm</u>, <u>finish</u> the <u>point</u> you're on and move on to your <u>conclusion</u>.

Stephanie never had a problem with keeping cool.

Treat an exam like a spa day — just relax...

Some people actually do lose the plot when they get into the exam. The trick is to keep calm and well... carry on. If you make sure you get your exam technique sorted, you'll be as relaxed as a sloth in a room full of easy chairs.

Section Six — Exam Advice

Sample Exam Question

And now the bit you've all been waiting for — a sample exam question and a lovely little plan.
Go and make yourself a cup of tea, then settle down and enjoy.

Here's a sample exam question...

Read this feisty exam question. That's the best way to start...

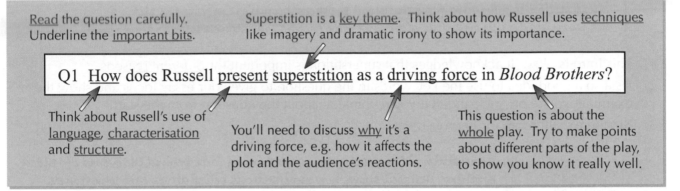

Read the question carefully. Underline the important bits.

Superstition is a key theme. Think about how Russell uses techniques like imagery and dramatic irony to show its importance.

Q1 How does Russell present superstition as a driving force in *Blood Brothers*?

Think about Russell's use of language, characterisation and structure.

You'll need to discuss why it's a driving force, e.g. how it affects the plot and the audience's reactions.

This question is about the whole play. Try to make points about different parts of the play, to show you know it really well.

Here's how you could plan your answer

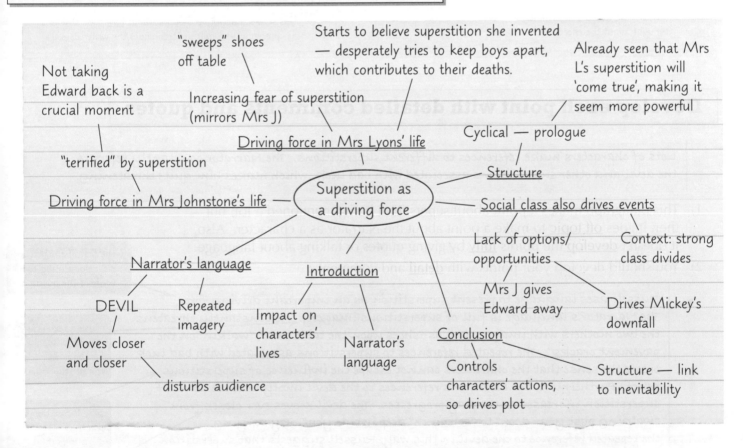

Not taking Edward back is a crucial moment

"sweeps" shoes off table

Starts to believe superstition she invented — desperately tries to keep boys apart, which contributes to their deaths.

Already seen that Mrs L's superstition will 'come true', making it seem more powerful

Increasing fear of superstition (mirrors Mrs J)

"terrified" by superstition

Driving force in Mrs Lyons' life

Cyclical — prologue

Driving force in Mrs Johnstone's life —

Superstition as a driving force

Structure

Social class also drives events

Narrator's language

Introduction

Lack of options/ opportunities

Context: strong class divides

DEVIL

Repeated imagery

Mrs J gives Edward away

Drives Mickey's downfall

Moves closer and closer

Impact on characters' lives

Narrator's language

Conclusion

disturbs audience

Controls characters' actions, so drives plot

Structure — link to inevitability

What do examiners eat? Why, egg-sam-wiches of course...

The most important thing to remember is DON'T PANIC. Take a deep breath, read the question, read it again, write a plan... take another deep breath... and start writing. Leave 5 minutes at the end to check your answer too.

Worked Answer

These pages will show you how to take an OK answer and turn it into a really good one that will impress the examiner.

Use your introduction to get off to a good start

These pages are all about how to word your sentences to impress the examiner, so we haven't included everything from the plan on page 59.

You might start with something like...

> Superstition is a driving force in 'Blood Brothers' because it affects the plot. It's particularly important as a driving force in Mrs Johnstone's life.

1) This intro is okay. It acknowledges that superstition is important for different reasons.

2) It's also a good idea to use the key words in the question to give your essay focus and show the examiner you're on track and that you're thinking about the question from the start.

3) But there's still room for improvement...

This intro gives a few brief examples, which will then form the paragraphs of the essay.

> Superstition is arguably the main driving force behind the events of 'Blood Brothers'. Russell shows how superstitious belief drives Mrs Johnstone's powerlessness, Mrs Lyons' descent into madness and, through the women's actions, the deaths of the twins. Throughout the play, Russell uses the Narrator as a dramatic device to remind the audience of the invented superstition and its eventual effect. This highlights how powerful and dangerous superstitious belief can be.

This shows the examiner that you've thought about the effects of techniques.

This shows that you've thought about how superstition is presented through the techniques the writer uses.

Develop each point with detailed comments and quotes

> Lots of characters make references to different superstitions. The Narrator constantly refers to the devil and other superstitions associated with bad luck, which makes him quite threatening.

1) This paragraph makes a point about superstition being mentioned a lot, but then it goes off topic to make a point about the Narrator as a character. Also, it doesn't develop the points fully by giving quotes or talking about language.

2) You should develop your points with detail and comments:

The first line makes a clear point using the words of the question.

> Russell uses language to present superstition as an important driving force. The Narrator's language is full of superstitious imagery. He constantly threatens the two mothers with images such as "shoes upon the table" and "walkin' on the pavement cracks". The repeated references to superstitions associated with bad luck create the sense that the characters cannot escape the influence of superstitious belief. Furthermore, the Narrator's references to the devil imply that the power of superstition increases as the play progresses. The devil moves ever closer, from "walking past your door" to "screamin' deep inside you". By varying the repeated reference to the devil in this way, Russell suggests that superstition is an important factor in driving the play towards its tragic ending.

Using technical terms to analyse language will help you get top marks.

Stay focused on the idea that superstition is important.

This keeps the paragraph focused on language.

Highlighting changes shows that you've thought about the play as a whole, not just one character or scene.

Worked Answer

You need to make a variety of points

Here's a point you could make about how superstition affects the <u>characters' lives</u>.

> Superstition is an important driving force in Mrs Johnstone's life. Her superstitious belief is made clear when she panics about the shoes on the table, and it continues throughout the play.

1) This paragraph has a good opening sentence, with a clear <u>point</u> related to the <u>question</u>.

2) However, you can improve it by discussing <u>quotes</u> and highlighting <u>important moments</u>:

Identifying the causes of important events shows that you understand the play.

> To some extent, the course of Mrs Johnstone's life is determined by her superstitious belief. It is a crucial factor in her leaving Edward with Mrs Lyons — she wants to take him back, but she is "terrified" by Mrs Lyons' invented superstition about twins separated at birth. This stage direction shows that Mrs Johnstone's belief is so strong that even a superstition she's never heard of can control her life.

Show the examiner that you've thought about different elements of the play.

3) You could develop this further by discussing another <u>theme</u> as a <u>counter argument</u>:

Some exam boards will give you marks for linking the play to its context.

> However, superstition is not the only driving force in Mrs Johnstone's life. Her decision to give Edward to Mrs Lyons is also motivated by social class. Her situation as a working-class, single mother prompts her to give Edward the chance of a life in a "palace" with "all his own toys". Russell uses the character of Mrs Johnstone to show how the strong class divides of late-twentieth-century Britain could be a powerful force in determining the course of people's lives.

Finish your essay in style

You could say:

> In conclusion, superstition is a driving force because it affects the characters in the play, and because it is a crucial factor in plot development.

1) This conclusion is okay, but it doesn't summarise <u>how</u> superstition is presented as a driving force.

2) So to make it really <u>impressive</u> you could say something like...

> Superstition is presented as a driving force in the characters' lives in 'Blood Brothers'. This is demonstrated by constant references to it in both dialogue and stage directions. Moreover, the overall structure of the play reflects the powerful nature of superstitious belief, since the consequences of Mrs Lyons' invented superstition are shown in a prologue. The twins are destined to arrive at this tragic end, and superstition proves to be a crucial factor in their deaths, as well as their lives.

If you think there's a technique — like structure — that really stands out as important, make sure you mention that.

Make your last sentence really stand out — it's your last opportunity to impress the examiner.

Why do alligators write good essays? Their quotes are snappy...

It seems like there's a lot to remember on these two pages, but there's not really. To summarise — write a scorching intro and a sizzling conclusion, make a good range of points (one per paragraph) and include plenty of examples. Easy.

Index

The Characters from 'Blood Brothers'

Phew! You should be an expert on *Blood Brothers* by now. But if you want a bit of light relief and a quick recap of the play's plot, sit yourself down and read through *Blood Brothers — The Cartoon*...

Mrs Johnstone

Mickey Johnstone

Edward Lyons

Mrs Lyons

Mr Lyons

Sammy Johnstone

Linda

Narrator

Willy Russell's 'Blood Brothers'